WHY THERE ARE NO GOOD MEN LEFT

ALSO BY BARBARA DAFOE WHITEHEAD

The Divorce Culture

WHY THERE ARE NO GOOD MEN LEFT

The Romantic Plight of the New Single Woman

BARBARA DAFOE WHITEHEAD

BROADWAY BOOKS | NEW YORK

A hardcover edition of this book was published
in 2003 by Broadway Books.

Book design by Richard Oriolo

The Library of Congress has cataloged the hardcover edition
as follows:

Whitehead, Barbara Dafoe, 1944–
Why there are no good men left: the romantic plight
of the new single woman /
Barbara Dafoe Whitehead
p.   cm.
Includes bibliographical references.
1. Women college graduates—United States—Social conditions.
2. Man-woman relationships—United States.
3. Dating (Social customs)—United States.   I. Title.
HQ1421 .W525 2003
306.7—dc21
2002027968

ISBN 9780767906401

146712470

*For Ralph, who introduced me
to the pleasures of romantic courtship*

". . . I am sick of them all. Thank Heaven! I am going to-morrow where I shall find a man who has not one agreeable quality, who has neither manner nor sense to recommend him. Stupid men are the only ones worth knowing, after all."

"Take care Lizzy; that speech savours strongly of disappointment."

—Jane Austen, *Pride and Prejudice*, 1813

CONTENTS

ACKNOWLEDGMENTS

Many people helped in the research and writing of this book.

I am deeply grateful to all the young women who are willing to take hours out of their busy lives to answer my questions about their school, work, and dating experiences. Special thanks to Martha Hardwick, Jennifer Tobriner, and Leslie Bywater for their help and sustained interest in the project.

My colleague and friend, Rutgers sociologist David Popenoe, has taught me much about marriage, divorce, and cohabitation trends. I am also grateful for his careful reading and comments on a draft of the book. Robert J. Lacey provided expert help with Census data. Theresa Kirby was an indispensable source of advice on how to track down articles and data on the Internet.

Members of my family were the first to inspire and encourage my interest in this topic. My daughters, Ann and Sarah, both working singles in their thirties, gave me insight into their generation's experience. My son, John, kept me mindful of the single male's side of the story. My sister-in-law, Mary Whitehead, gave me invaluable professional assistance in conceptualizing, developing, and piloting the interview study. My brother, Richard Dafoe, genereously provided office space for several interviews and kept me entertained and well fed during my stay in Dallas. My husband, Ralph, served as counselor, critic, and in-house editor.

My thanks to Suzanne Oakes for seeing merit in my ideas, and especially to my editor, Kristine Puopolo, for her good sense and tactful advice. I am ever grateful to my agents, Glen Hartley and Lynn Chu, for their expert guidance and faithful support over the years.

THE ROMANTIC
PLIGHT OF THE NEW
SINGLE WOMAN

THIS BOOK IS ABOUT A CONTEMPORARY crisis in dating and mating. It explains why some of the best educated and most accomplished young single women in society today are discontented with their love lives, why romantic disappointment has emerged as a generational theme, and why many of these women have come to believe that "there are no good men left."

Finding lasting love is never easy, but it seems to be especially hard for women today. Evidence of their romantic frustration is everywhere: in popular television shows like *Will & Grace* and *Sex and the*

City; in the gargantuan appetite for self-help dating and relationships books; in the endless talkfests about men's frailties and failings; in the hit movies and bestselling novels about 30-something single women's search for Mr. Right; in a crop of articles and books on how to get over being dumped; in the explosion of Internet sites devoted to the search for love. Youth used to be the season of romantic love. Seemingly, it is now becoming the season of romantic discontent.

Much of the frustration is expressed in the popular perception that "there are no good men left." This sentiment is not an attack on men as a gender. Far from it. More than at any other time in history, today's young women enjoy warm friendships, collegial work relationships, and common life experiences with men. Nor is it a lament about men's unavailability as lovers and boyfriends. Young women are able to find men who are available and ready for sex or for a relationship. But what the sentiment does reflect is their view of how difficult it is to find the *right* man at the *right time* in their lives.

For women today, the search for love is fraught with uncertainty. The dating world is full of chaos and confusion. No one knows what the rules, conventions, or accepted practices are. No consensus exists on crucial matters of romantic conduct such as who should take the initiative in dating, when to have sex, when to live together, what it means to be a couple, who proposes marriage, what constitutes commitment, how to go about finding a worthy marriage partner, and what it takes to make love last. No one is even sure about the right way to break up. All of these matters are contested, debated, and up for grabs.

Moreover, it is hard to know where to find suitable single men. Once women tire of going out to clubs and bars, there are few public spots where they can go to meet men. And as work consumes more of everyone's time, private entertaining has dwindled as well. Young singles are often left out of parties hosted by married couples. So ready-made social occasions to meet single men at private parties are not easy to come by.

Further complicating the situation, young women find little social support or sympathy for their romantic ambitions outside of their immediate family and friends. In the media and popular culture, they've heard nothing but gloomy predictions and forecasts of failure. They've been told that their chances for marriage are almost gone by the time they reach 30. They've been reminded of the high rate of divorce. They've been instructed in the gendered nature of human mating behavior, the persistence of conflict in dating relationships, and the utterly irreconcilable differences between men and women. When a Gallup survey of Gen-Xers revealed that both men and women were searching for soul mates, baby-boom pundits responded exasperatedly by telling the younger generation to "get real." It is easy to understand why young single women, now in the prime years for finding their soul mates, would be disheartened about their chances for realizing their hopes and dreams.

Among these accomplished young women, the uncertainty about their chances for finding lasting love stands in sharp contrast to their otherwise optimistic and buoyant outlook. This generation of college-educated women has come of age at a time of unparalleled opportunity and freedom for women, a time when the doors to the classroom and the locker room have swung wide open, when traditional sexual constraints on women have been loosened or come undone, when their opportunities for education, employment, and personal development seem nearly boundless. These opportunities have given them the poise, confidence, and choices that make it possible for them to lead full, exciting, independent lives.

The young women I've met and interviewed for this book express a high level of confidence when it comes to their ability to be successful in their chosen work, or at least to acquire the educational and professional opportunities for success. To be sure, their early career experiences are not without reversals and setbacks, but they feel well prepared to enter the world of work. They've been readied for the challenges of the work world since their early school years. When I ask them to rank their confidence in their ability to achieve their future career goals on a scale of one to ten, their confidence meter registers at a nine or ten. When it comes to their love lives, however, it's a different story. When I ask about their confidence in their ability to achieve their future romantic goals, many drop their ranking to a five or six.

A friend of mine, a teacher at a Midwestern college, routinely gives her women students a list of problems and asks them to rank the items on the list according to their own views of what poses the greatest obstacle to women today. The items include job discrimination, sexual harassment in the workplace, and domestic violence. But what most often surfaces as the number one obstacle cited by her students is another item on the list—"finding and keeping a loving partner."

Even the language young women use to describe their love lives can sound strangely flat and passionless. Much of the rhetoric of true love is missing. A classical language of romance, rooted in poetry, literature, and art, has been supplanted by a scientized "relationships talk." When young women recount their experiences with boyfriends, they rarely use expressions like "falling in love" or "being in love" or "finding the love of my life." Instead of love, they talk fluently about sexual needs, "being in a relationship," and "issues" of communication, intimacy, and commitment. Marriage is a word they use timidly, or ironically, perhaps because they've been warned that talk of marriage can seem needy or desperate. Even romantic disappointment has lost its association with grand passion. Breakups are spoken of matter-of-factly as "dumpings."

Such perfunctory talk of relationships is not a sign that young women have given up on romantic love, however. There are moments when you catch a note of wistful desire in their stories. Some women still refer to their first boyfriend as "my one true love," and they seem almost shy when they say it. Others recall, as one of their favorite movie moments, the Romeo and Juliet scene in the movie *Say Anything*, when John Cusack holds up his boom box and serenades Ione Skye in a desperate, go-for-broke declaration of love. But somehow the experience of such pure romantic ambition is missing from their own boyfriend stories, or when it appears, it is often twisted into some form of weirdness, like stalking or obsession.

Most of all, young women express bewilderment about how and when they will find the right person to marry. Of course, not every woman chooses to be married, and happily, women today don't have to be married in order to lead full, successful, and satisfying lives in the social mainstream. Also, single women are not necessarily unpartnered. Today's young women enjoy a wide range of choice in their intimate relationships. They are freer than women in the past to affirm and act upon the truth that the realm of human affection encompasses more than heterosexual marriage and children. And because well-educated women now enjoy greater economic independence and more life options, they do not have to "settle" for a less than desirable mate simply to fulfill social expectations or out of sheer economic necessity.

Nevertheless, given this welcome new range of life options, the one that most young single women now freely aspire to is marriage and children—or so recent statistically reliable evidence strongly suggests. According to virtually every poll and survey conducted on the subject, the vast majority of young women say that they want to be married someday. What's more, they place a very high priority on this life goal.[1] In a 2001 survey by the Gallup Organization, single women, ages 20 to 29 were asked how important it was to them to have a good marriage and family life. Among the four choices (extremely important, quite important, somewhat important, or not important), 89 percent chose extremely important.[2]

These women know that they can fulfill their desire for children on their own initiative, if necessary. Changes in social attitudes and policies have made it possible and acceptable for well-educated, employed women to bear or adopt children on their own. From assisted reproduction to adoption services to health insurance coverage, medical treatment and institutional supports are available for unmarried women who want to become mothers. More than half of college-educated women in their 20s (53.7 percent) say that it is okay for a woman to have a child on her own if the right man doesn't come along in time.[3] Some have already considered default plans for motherhood if they are still unmarried by their late 30s. Though they may never resort to these plans, they nevertheless see motherhood as a life goal that they can achieve on their own initiative, if they choose.

It's not the same when it comes to fulfilling their desire for marriage. Finding a suitable marriage mate requires the reciprocal consent, public commitment, and active participation of a second party. But in fact, it goes beyond a second party. It usually involves third parties who have some interest or stake in the match. Indeed, the participation of interested third parties is what distinguishes human mate selection from the mating behavior of other species. And the purpose of third-party involvement is to help the first party and the second party engage in a process of mutual selection.

All of this is another way of saying that the successful search for a life mate is a social, as well as individual, pursuit. Mating, or to put it in more culturally specific terms, romantic courtship, has customarily relied on social supports as well as individual efforts. Providing a system for successful mate selection is one of the fundamental tasks of a society. Indeed, the task of pairing off men and women for the purposes of sex, marriage, and childbearing is so important that no known society leaves mate selection and marriage up to lone individuals roaming around on their own. Yet this often seems to be exactly what many single women today have to do.

In the popular culture, there is little cheer or hope. The portrait of mating is bleak. From novels to self-help literature to popular studies of gender relations, a romantic vision of youthful love has been displaced by a pseudoscientific portrait of mating behavior and misbehavior. One influential school of popular thought draws heavily and crudely on the theories of evolutionary psychology. It sees love as a battlefield, a world marked by conflict, deception, and manipulation. According to this school, men and women's psyches are hardwired to seek different reproductive goals—he wants sex with many partners and she wants babies with one partner. Given such different goals, men and women pursue different mating strategies. Men seek to have sex with lots of women with minimal investment of time and money in any one woman, and women seek resources from one man while withholding sexual favors from lots of men. These strategies obviously clash, and, for that reason, human mating behavior is filled with gender strife—or perhaps milder forms of Mars/Venus miscommunication. And since the hard-wiring is here to stay, there's not much anyone can do but become a skilled combatant in sexual warfare.

A second school of popular thought, heavily dominated by

self-help literature, points the finger at women themselves. Women's problems in mating aren't the result of hard-wiring, this school suggests. They are the result of soft-headedness. According to this body of popular opinion and advice, women need only look in the mirror to understand why they are unhappy with their love lives. Their dating problems are self-made and their wounds self-inflicted. These critics charge that women are guilty of misreading men's behavior. As a result, they are either too giving or too self-absorbed, too needy or too independent, too demanding or not demanding enough, too emotionally controlling or too emotionally out of control. Perhaps the most common critique of women's dating behavior resurrects an old question, first raised by John Bunyan's Mr. Badman in *Pilgrim's Progress*: "Who would keep a cow of their own that can have a quart of milk for a penny?" Today's women are too sexually obliging, according to this view, and they are giving men too many privileges without asking for anything in return.

Yet, as popular as these explanations may be, neither truly illuminates the contemporary situation for women or answers the questions: Why is this happening now? Why is it happening to this group of accomplished women? The hardwired school of thought stresses the aspects of mating behavior that develop across long periods of time—not mere decades or centuries or millennia—but eons. Yet the pervasive sense of romantic discontent experienced by many young women today is a recent development. Presumably, our hardwiring hasn't changed so drastically in such a short period of time. But clearly something has changed.

The "soft-headed" school of thought focuses on individual women's behavior, but it fails to explain why so many young women seem to be afflicted with difficulties in finding a mate. To be sure, there are women whose sexual or dating behavior could stand some criticism and correction. However, the contemporary mood of romantic disenchantment is not limited to sexually promiscuous or neurotically needy young women. In fact, there are plenty of sexually conservative women who "aren't giving away the milk for free," but who are just as discouraged by their search for a suitable man to marry as the women who are behaving like sexual dairy queens. Something more widespread is going on.

THIS BOOK OFFERS A DIFFERENT explanation of women's romantic plight. It looks beyond the evolutionary behavior of the species and beyond the idiosyncrasies of individual dating behavior to a neglected middle ground between the two: namely, what's been happening in society. It focuses on two social changes in particular. One is the rise of a new kind of single woman, with a new timetable for her early adult years. The other is the upheaval in the mating system. Each of these changes is recent. Each is historically significant. Together, these changes are altering the course and landscape of love.

For today's young single woman, there is a new life pattern in the early adult years. It places a premium on education, personal growth, and early career development. She completes a four-year degree. She then goes on to graduate or professional school or enters the world of work, possibly to return to school a few years later. If she is marriage-minded, she doesn't begin to focus on marriage until she reaches her late 20s. For the college-educated women of the baby boom generation, the common sequence was to marry and then to seek satisfying work. For today's young college-educated women, however, the sequence has been reversed: first comes satisfying work and then the search for a suitable life partner.

This new pattern is clearly evident in the demographic trends. College-educated women are staying single longer. In 1970, the median age of entry into a first marriage for women was not yet 21 (20.8). Today, it has reached 25, the oldest level in a century.[4] In the past, college-educated women have married about a year and a half later than other women, and that gap may have increased in recent years. So today's college women may be at least 27 when they tie the knot.[5]

Thus, there has been a dramatic rise in the percentage of single women in their 20s and 30s. The proportion of women, ages 20 to 24, who had never married doubled between 1970 and 2000, from 36 percent to 73 percent, and tripled for women, ages 30 to 34, from 6 percent to 22 percent. (Changes were similar for men. For example, the proportion of men, ages 20 to 24, who had never married increased from 55 percent in 1970 to 84 percent in 2000. The proportion of men, ages 30 to 34, who had never married increased from 9 percent to 30 percent over the same time period.)[6]

There has also been a change in the conduct of young women's intimate lives. Though today's young women are delaying their entry into marriage, they are not waiting to have sex until they are approaching, or have reached, their wedding day. The average age of first sexual intercourse is 17, leaving an interval of eight or more years between first sex and first marriage. Moreover, women's early sexual relationships are less likely to be connected to the expectation or promise of marriage than they were in the past. Since the sexual revolution of the '60s, the cultural meaning and purpose of sex in an unmarried young woman's life have changed. Increasingly, early sexual experience has become part of a normative process of adolescent self-development rather than an initiatory event that is closely linked to the timing of first marriage. Similarly, romantic relationships in the early adult years are not necessarily connected to marriage. During college, and in the years immediately following college graduation, young women regard their intimate partnerships as a way of discovering more about themselves and what they want in a future life partner rather than as a hunt for a husband. Likewise, there has been a change in the first living-together union. For the vast majority of young women in past generations, the first living-together union was marriage. Today, it is cohabitation. The majority of young women today will live with a boyfriend before they live with a husband.[7]

Thus, the timetable for the new single woman combines an emphasis on early career development with a slower march to the altar. During this stage of early adulthood, she spends a prolonged period of time as a single woman, living and working on her own, and engaging in intimate partnerships of varying seriousness and duration. Before she seriously seeks a life partner, she seeks to establish a life of her own.

Along with the advent of this new timetable, a second recent change has occurred. It is a historic upheaval in the long-established mating system. For most of the past century, there was one dominant mating system. It could be accurately described as a system of romantic courtship and marriage. It was devoted almost solely to the young and never-married. Its main function was to pair up young people, usually while one or both of them were still in school, and move them toward marriage, usually in the years shortly after the end of formal schooling. This goal was accomplished for the majority of young women in society. As recently as 1970, a scant 10.5 percent of all women aged 25 to 29 were never married.[8]

During the first two-thirds of the 20th century, the romantic courtship component of this system governed the dating behavior of young people. As cultural historian Beth L. Bailey has argued, this system was so broad and comprehensive that it could be described as national in its scope and influence. It provided a set of rules, conventions, and practices that nearly everyone recognized and many followed. As Bailey writes: "The rules were constantly reiterated and reinforced. The sameness of the message was overwhelming. Popular magazines, advice and etiquette books, texts used in high school and college marriage courses, the professional journals of educators who taught the courses, all formed a remarkably coherent universe."[9] Though these rules may seem narrow and stifling to us today, she observes, at the time they provided a clear and coherent guide to dating and mating. No one suffered confusion about what the standards for courtship were, or what the consequences for violating the standards might be.

Moreover, this national pattern was supported by a social infrastructure. In the 20th century, romantic courtship was closely linked to the most youth-oriented social institution outside of the family: namely, the school. Dating was anchored in a school population, school social life, and an increasingly leisured adolescent peer culture. As coeducational higher education grew in the 20th century, the college became increasingly influential as the educational institution that shaped and elaborated the social rules and rituals of courtship. At the same time, parents and other adults indirectly supported and sustained this system. Parents exerted influence over the mating choices of their offspring by steering them into a college where they were likely to date and marry someone of similar background. Faculty and administrators supervised collegiate social life *in loco parentis*.

This courtship pattern, and the social machinery that sustained it, was so well developed and commonly accepted that there was a sense of transparency and "naturalness" about the selection of a life partner. Falling in love seemed to be one of the reliable features of college life, and romantic love in college was connected closely to aspirations for marriage. Most men and women expected to be married shortly after college, and for many women, that meant that they would be pinned or engaged by their senior year in college.

By the time that the women who are now in their 20s and 30s reached college, this national courtship system, for all practical purposes, no longer existed. Similarly, the campus-based social infrastructure supporting this courtship system had disappeared. The college had ceased to function as a marriage market for women; the college years had ceased to be the prime time for finding a marriage mate; and campus social life had ceased to be organized around couple dating. The tradition of *in loco parentis* had vanished altogether.

In recent years, a new mating system has been emerging. It is not a romantic courtship and marriage system. It is designed to foster the romantic pursuits, not so much of the young, but of an older universe of dating singles. This universe is highly diverse. It includes senior citizens, the divorced, never-married single parents, gays and lesbians, as well as young never-marrieds. And like its universe, the purposes of this emerging mating system are more diverse: it is designed for a variety of intimate pair-bonded arrangements, from marriage to living together to serial monogamy to sexual partnerings without any strings attached. This emerging mating system has no comprehensive "national" set of standards for romantic courtship. Nor is it likely that it ever will, given its diversity.

In many respects, the emerging system offers advantages over the earlier system. It is open to a much broader population. It is responsive to the social trends that have created a larger and healthier older population of widowed or divorced singles. It is inclusive of homosexual, as well as heterosexual, couples. And it enshrines the principles of freedom of choice in private intimate arrangements. The emerging mating system doesn't judge love; it treats it as a matter of equal opportunity for all. At the same time, however, this system has a drawback for the marriage-minded young woman. It doesn't privilege her desire for marriage or provide any coherent set of widely accepted practices or conventions to help her achieve her goals.

The new single woman who hopes to marry someday faces a quandary: she isn't able to rely on the earlier courtship system. It no longer exists. Even if it did, it wouldn't fit the timetable of her early adult life. It was designed for college women who got married in their early 20s. And the emerging system doesn't offer an updated courtship system that helps her fulfill her aspirations for finding a life mate at an older age. What today's new single woman needs—but doesn't have yet—is a contemporary courtship pattern that fits her timetable and supports her efforts to make a successful choice of a life mate.

However, that may be changing. Socially innovative approaches to mate selection are appearing. Women are regaining some sense of coherence and control over their own romantic lives. They are taking a more focused, organized, and professional approach to the search for love itself. Some women are turning to the habits, tools, and technologies of the workplace in order to conduct a search. They are using the savvy and skills that got them ahead in the work world to help reach their goals in the world of love.

THOUGH THE ROMANTIC PURSUITS of today's new single woman have been lavishly documented in the popular culture, they have gotten far less attention from the scholarly world. On this aspect of women's intimate lives, the social science research is thin. Except for studies of dating violence and cohabitation, there are remarkably few studies on the actual dating and mating behavior of today's young working singles. There are several reasons why this is so: once women leave the catchment area of the college campus, it is harder to study and track them over time. Also, it is expensive and time-consuming to undertake any kind of large-scale, nationally representative study of a population of young dating singles. And finally, because the new patterns influencing the love lives of young women are so recent, it will be a while before researchers can conduct the fieldwork, gather the statistics, analyze the data, and develop a full picture of contemporary patterns of mating and dating. In the meantime, any effort to make sense of what is happening in the dating world today will necessarily take the form of a preliminary sketch rather than a finished portrait.

I have drawn this sketch in broad brush strokes. In doing so, I have relied on a wide variety of sources, including personal interviews, focus group discussions, national surveys, demographic studies, histories of dating and mating, and popular fiction. I've consulted self-help literature on relationships and surveyed the vast universe of online and offline relationship advice. (On the Internet alone, a Google search for "relationships advice" turns up more than 1.7 million entries.) I have also drawn upon recent research conducted by the National Marriage Project at Rutgers, where I serve as co-director. This research includes recent qualitative studies of young singles, as well as a 2001 national survey on dating and mating attitudes, conducted by the Gallup Organization and based on a nationally representative sample of men and women, ages 20 to 29. Unless otherwise noted, survey findings in this book come from that national study.

In addition, through structured interviews, I have gathered the school, work, and dating histories of 60 single women between the ages of 22 to 40, most in their late 20s and early 30s. I was fortunate to have found so many engaging young women to interview. Virtually without exception, the women who shared their personal histories were highly educated, analytically sophisticated, lively, funny, thoughtful, and engaged by the topic. Most of the women were white, but the group also included Asian, African-American, and Hispanic women. About half of those I interviewed had graduated from the Ivies and a handful of other elite schools like Wesleyan, Stanford, Johns Hopkins, the University of Chicago, and the University of Virginia, while the rest had college degrees from good private colleges and public universities. Quite a few had earned graduate or professional degrees, in such fields as engineering, law, and business. At the time of the interviews, most of the women were living and working in major metropolitan areas across the nation. (Their individual stories appear throughout the book, though their names and certain identifying details have been changed.)

Yet insightful as these accomplished young women were about many aspects of their experience, they turned out to be as mystified about the reasons for their dating discontents as I was at the outset. They had lots of shrewd observations on the dating scene, a wealth of opinions, theories, and speculations about relationships, and wry commentary on their own love lives, but no revelatory insights. One or two observed that they felt like pioneers in the domain of love. Because their early adult life paths were so different from those of prior generations of women, they had no role models or relevant experience to guide them.

As it turned out, it was the novels piling up on my nightstand that provided the earliest and most valuable clues into the social origins of young women's romantic plight. Beginning in the 1990s, a popular fiction emerged, and with it a new kind of serio-comic character. She is the romantically disconsolate, endlessly self-monitoring single woman who has embarked on a desperate, sometimes obsessive, search for a good man. Pam Houston was one of the first to introduce this character in two collections of short stories published in the early 1990s. Helen Fielding's *Bridget Jones's Diary* (1996) made the 30-something singleton a familiar stereotype, and a raft of lookalike novels soon followed in the late '90s. I've counted more than 30 novels based on the Bridget Jones formula, and each season brings several more. Even Harlequin Books, famous for bodice-ripping romances, has joined the trend with a series of books dedicated to the young single woman's romantic plight.

Critics dismissively dubbed this fiction Chick Lit, but I tried to give it a closer look. After all, this was a popular literature written mainly by 30-something women; it enjoyed enormous popularity among the reading audience of women in their 20s and 30s, and it appeared contemporaneously with the rising number of educated single young women in society. Chick Lit could not be read as a documentary description of women's love lives, of course; many of the novels were cartoonish, spoofy, and raunchy. But the emergence of this literature in the '90s was a revealing cultural signal that something had gone awry in the love lives of young singles.

Moreover, as I read this formulaic fiction, I was struck by two of its distinguishing features. One was the character of the young woman herself. In classic romantic fiction, the unmarried woman fits into one of three types: a virginal maiden, a lusty widow, or a dessicated old maid. The single woman in these novels resembles none of the above. She is a woman in her late 20s or early 30s, educated, independent, sexually liberated, and living and working on her own.

I also noted a second feature: the heroine is isolated from a set-tled social world. Her romantic pursuits are disconnected from any larger public or even family concerns. In the romantic tradition, the story of lovers requires the presence, and often the opposition, of some important family or social group. It's hard to imagine Romeo and Juliet without the feuding Montagues and Capulets. However, in this popular fiction, the heroine is cut off from the larger social world. With the possible exception of a bossy mother and a gay friend, she finds herself all alone in a bewildering environment. She is lost and disoriented. What she needs is a map, compass, or guide, but she doesn't have one. She has to figure out how to reach her romantic destination entirely on her own.

Slight as these works might be from a literary standpoint, it seemed to me that they contained an important sociological insight. They pointed to a new kind of woman and a new kind of mating sys-tem. Chick Lit raised the possibility that more than mere failure and resentment lay behind the sentiment that "there are no good men left." It pointed to more far-reaching social changes that have changed the search for love itself.

THE BOOK BEGINS WITH A PORTRAIT of the women and their plight, as represented in their own life stories. It then turns to the broader changes in the organization of young women's early adult lives and in the courtship and mating system itself that have come together. Next, it provides a map to the contemporary mating land-scape and identifies some of the challenges to a successful search. Finally, it considers what a contemporary courtship system for the new single woman might look like and what we can do to create it.

I wrote this book in order to gain a better understanding of what was happening to inspire a widespread sense of anxiety and confusion about mating and marriage among young educated women. But I had a second purpose in mind as well. I wanted to provide an alternative perspective to the two views that have so commonly been offered to young women.

In recent times, single women have been told "you can't have it all." Instead, they have been given two stark choices. One is "get married early, or risk being barren." The other is "get married late, or risk going barefoot." Each admonition contains a useful caution. The "marry early" school of thought underscores the problems of delaying childbearing until older ages. The "marry late" school of thought emphasizes the fact that a high divorce rate makes marriage untrustworthy as a source of economic security for women. Still, these opposing options are equally unappealing. They represent a retreat from the vision of a woman's life that has a satisfying combination of love and work, of private and public achievement. It is easy to understand why single women who are now on the threshold of the time in life when they are in their prime years of mate selection and marriage would be dispirited by both options.

Moreover, each imposes a tyranny of the clock. The "marry early or be barren" school asks women to obey their biological clock or risk losing out on children. The "marry late or go barefoot" school requires women to obey their career clock or risk economic insecurity. Neither credits, let alone offers any help or support for, women who want to combine work, marriage, and children.

The argument of this book is that it is possible to have both satisfying work and lasting love, but in order to achieve these goals, it is first necessary to be mindful of how social forces have changed the timetable and course of love. Early on in my interviews, I was struck by how so many smart young women had so little useful knowledge to guide them and to help them understand the new dating environment. For one thing, they had little awareness of the social realities that influence the timing and choice of a marriage partner. They know a lot about the realities of other high-stakes selection processes—how to choose a college or a career path, for example—but they aren't as well versed in how to go about finding the person they will spend their lives with. For another, some had an expectation that they would find their soul mate serendipitously, the way people do in the movies. But it rarely works that way in real life. In western societies where people choose their own marriage mates, rather than having others make the choice for them, much is left to individual taste and imagination. However, the search for a mate is not simply an individual pursuit, much less a matter of fate or randomness. Our choices in love, as in other areas of our lives, are structured by social influences. We are bound by our place in time and space as well as by social class, law, custom, and technology to a set of identifiable patterns and practices in our choice of a mate. If these social influences are undergoing recent and dramatic change, then it is important to understand how and why.

Such knowledge won't necessarily get you a date for Friday night or a marriage proposal, but it can be, to use an overused word, empowering. You are less likely to act on mistaken assumptions. You can avoid wasted time and needless anxiety. You can make wiser, more informed choices. You can avoid needless heartbreak. You can resist the tyranny of the clocks. With a better sense of the social landscape, you can gain a greater sense of confidence and control over the conduct and course of your love life.

CHAPTER I

DATING MR. NOT READY

CHRISTINA IS 31, SLIM, PRETTY, a younger and darker-haired Annette Bening. The daughter of a professor and an artist, she grew up in a family where books, politics, and international sabbaticals filled her early life. After attending an elite boarding school in New England, she went off to college where she got interested in women's political issues and began to work in campaigns. In the years following college, she moved into progressively more responsible jobs as a fund raiser for Democratic women candidates and causes. At the time we meet, she is working as the director of an international relations consulting group with an income in the high five figures. Yet there's one nagging source of discontent in her otherwise contented and accomplished life. As we chat over plates of mushroom ragout in a trendy Washington restaurant, she says ruefully: "I'm always getting involved with Mr. Not Ready."

Christina's last Mr. Not Ready was someone she thought she might end up marrying. They were in a relationship for three years. She followed him from the West Coast to Washington so that they could be together, and soon after they moved in together. But only a short time later, she regretted the decision. It turned out that her boyfriend needed extensive house training. Their story was *Pygmalion* in reverse. Instead of *My Fair Lady*, it was My Fair Laddie. She had to teach him, improve him, get him up to speed. It was exhausting.

Plus, he wasn't a very fast learner. When they first moved in together, they agreed to divide the housework equally. In the kitchen, they decided, she would cook and he would clean up. But he didn't live up to his part of the deal. "He pretended to do dishes," she says, bristling with fresh indignation. "I would come into the kitchen the next morning and find dishes still sitting there in cold, greasy water." After three months, she had had enough of his helplessness, feigned or otherwise. She dumped him. He still called from time to time to ask for her advice. But she was sick of being his mother and mentor.

Then, to her annoyance and dismay, she found out that her Mr. Not Ready had turned into Mr. Ready. With someone else! He was ready to make commitments to his new girlfriend. Ready to follow her to another state where she had a job. Ready to give her an engagement ring. She had spent three years of her life in a relationship that

she thought would lead to marriage or at least to a long-term relationship. She had trained the guy. And now her investment was paying off for someone else.

Even more depressingly, Christina's women friends were vanish-
ing into marriages. Her social life seemed to be dedicated to going
to parties for soon-to-be-married girlfriends. Each year passed with
another round of bridal showers, bachelor girl bashes, weddings, and
receptions, until finally Christina realized that she was being seated
at the cousins' table at weddings. If that weren't reminder enough of
her lack of romantic success, her mother kept asking why she
wasn't married yet. Christina panicked. She decided to take a break
from relationships to give herself time to de-stress, to get therapy,
and to think about what she really wanted to do with her life. She
gave up dating for a year.

All this happened just as Christina turned 30. By that age, she
had expected to be married herself. Instead, she had already been in
and out of relationships with seven different Mr. Not Readys. Her
heart had been broken four times. It didn't make sense. Here she
was, a woman who set goals for herself, met deadlines, accomplished
all the things on her professional "To Do" list, and yet she had
missed a major "To Do" in her life.

What made Christina's situation even more perplexing was that
she seemed to have all the qualifications for romantic success. She
was pretty, smart, and accomplished. She worked out and stayed in
shape. She was independent. It wasn't as if she were looking for
someone to take care of her. Maybe she came across as a little intim-
idating, but the right kind of guy should be attracted to her confidence and competence, shouldn't he? Yet, clearly, something was
wrong. At 30, her job resumé looked a lot more impressive than her

romantic resumé. Time after time, it seemed, she'd been promoted in work and pink-slipped in love.

CHRISTINA IS ONE OF THOSE perfectionist, pulled-together, Type A young women who can make other women, even those like me who are nearly twice her age, feel slightly discombobulated and disarrayed, as if we might have lipstick on our teeth or sleep in our eyes. She exudes confidence and control. Yet despite her crisp look and executive manner, she becomes younger and softer as she talks about her romantic desires. She is a woman who can do practically anything she wants on her own, but she doesn't want to be alone for her entire life. Though she's dedicated herself to feminist causes, she isn't hostile to men or marriage, like some professional feminists of the '60s. She isn't looking for a man to take care of her, but she wants to find a man who will care about her and share her life.

When Christina was in her early 20s, she didn't think much about how to find someone to marry. She knew that she wanted to be married someday but she wasn't ready to jump into such a big commitment at that point in her life. She needed to accomplish some things for herself and gain some life experience before settling down. Her parents had married at a young age, and their marriage didn't last. So she wanted to be mature enough to make a wise choice.

At 31, after taking a year's sabbatical from relationships, she decided to focus on the search for a husband. By now, she knows what she is looking for. Her standards are high but certainly not impossible: she wants to find a man who is physically attractive and takes good care of his body, enjoys his career but isn't career-obsessed, pursues interests outside of his work life and isn't boring, and dedicates himself to being faithful, loving, and kind. But finding

such a man is turning out to be more difficult than she once imag-
ined. For one thing, true love doesn't happen as naturally or
inevitably as she once thought. Up until the time she turned 30,
Christina believed that finding someone to marry was the one thing
in her life that she didn't have to work at or plan for. She thought that
Mr. Right would come along in the natural course of events. But that
hasn't happened, and she isn't sure how to make it happen.

A NEW LIFE STAGE

WOMEN LIKE CHRISTINA BARELY existed just a few decades
ago. In 1960, a college-educated woman who was in her late 20s or
early 30s, and "still single" as she would have been described back
then, was a rarity. She represented a miniscule 1.6 percent of all
women ages 25 to 34. In the entire country at the time, there were only
185,000 such women, a population roughly the size of the current population of Fort Wayne, Indiana. Today, however, she's become a far
more prominent figure on the social map. College-educated singles
now make up 28 percent of all women ages 25 to 34. Their numbers
have risen to 2.3 million, equal to the population of four Bostons. [1]

This new single woman has emerged in greater numbers as the
result of a confluence of two social trends. One is later age of entry
into first marriage. Young women today are marrying at older ages
than at any time in the past century. Moreover, the most dramatic
changes in the age of first marriage have occurred in recent decades.
Thus, over the past 30 years, the proportion of women who are single during the traditional "marrying years" has risen dramatically.
Between 1970 and 2000, the proportion of unmarried women ages

20 to 24 has doubled, and among those 30 to 34, the proportion has tripled. [2]

The second demographic trend is the dramatic increase in college attainment among young women. Historically, men have vastly outnumbered women in institutions of higher learning. (The sole exception, of course, is women's colleges.) Even as recently as 1960, women made up a modest 35 percent of that year's college graduating class. Today, however, women make up 56 percent of the most recent college graduating class. With these two trends, a growing population of young, college-educated women are spending a prolonged period of their early adult lives as working singles, out on their own.

It is a convention among social scientists to refer to this trend as a "postponement" of marriage. Their use of the term is accurate as a description of changes in the timing of entry into first marriage. But it can be misleading to the lay person. For it seems to suggest that the change is occurring wholly at the discretion of the young women themselves. To speak of the rise in the proportion of never-married young women as the "postponement" of marriage creates the impression that nothing has changed for them but the date of the wedding. It suggests that women are simply penciling in a later date for the cake and the caterer. If that were so, then the answer to the romantic frustrations of today's young women would be for them simply to pencil in an earlier date—that is, to return to the earlier pattern of marrying at younger ages and to count on men to return to it as well. But this is not the conclusion to be drawn from reports of the "postponement" of marriage.

The changing timetable for first marriage reflects larger changes in the early life course of educated young women. New patterns of schooling and work, as well as the changes in sexual and living-together partnerships, have created a new stage of life that comes between school and marriage for this generation of young women. This new stage of life reorganizes the traditional sequence of love and work in early adulthood. Whereas the baby boom generation of college-educated women married and then tried to find satisfying work, this generation of college-educated women is seeking satisfying work before trying to find someone to marry.

Following college graduation, young women's early adult life course follows a distinctive pattern. During their early 20s, they work very hard at getting established in careers. They vie for places with creative agencies, innovative companies, or prestige institutions, or they pursue a professional degree. They look for apartments in neighborhoods with a core cluster of upscale shops, including whole food markets, a Peet's or Starbucks, an independent bookstore, ethnic restaurants, and a health club. The competition for such places in many cities is intense. Some women have to audition for slots in an established house of young singles, leaving their names and cell phone numbers on sign-up sheets and hoping to be called back for a final interview. They strive for the image of "pulled-together" professionals, throwing out their Old Navy stuff and adopting an Ann Taylor uniform. Dark pantsuit. Small gold earrings. Black pumps. They pursue physical perfection. They join a gym and treadmill after work. And somewhere along this strenuous path to success, in between work and working out, they hope to find someone to "be in a relationship with."

In the years following college graduation, their first priority is individual financial independence. Both men and women seek to establish themselves as economically self-sufficient and stable at this stage in life. Eighty-six percent of never-married men and women ages 20 to 29 agree that it is extremely important to them to be "economically set" before they marry, according to the Gallup survey for the National Marriage Project. For many young adults, being "economically set" means paying off college loans, getting a professional job, and even buying a house. In addition, they have a strong desire for personal freedom and experience. As one woman told me, "I want to experience everything twice, once for myself and then again, with my future husband."

And finally, among young adults, there is the pervasive fear of divorce. The generation that has come of age during the divorce revolution has now reached early adulthood, and its members are all too aware of the fragile stage of marriage. A large majority (82 percent) agree that it is unwise for a woman to trust marriage as a reliable economic partnership. The high divorce rate is another reason for women's determination to invest in portable assets, like education and career, rather than to place their trust in the economic security of a long-lasting marriage. And young adults rightly believe that it is better to marry somewhat later if you want the marriage to last. One of the most reliable predictors of divorce is age at first marriage. People who marry in their teens have a dramatically higher risk of divorce than people who marry in their 20s. One recent study by a prominent demographer finds the single most important factor accounting for the recent leveling off of divorce rates is the rise in the median age of first marriage.[3]

In response to all these factors, women say that they are seeking "a life" before they look for a life partner. In the years immediately following college, they are no more ready than their male peers to make serious commitments. They have personal and career goals they want to accomplish before they begin to think about marriage.

"If my knight in shining armor came along right now," one 23-year-old engineer told me, "it would really screw up my life plan." When I repeat her observation to a 30-something single woman, she gives it a slightly different spin: "For all I know, my knight in shining armor could have come along when I was in my early 20s. But if he had, I wouldn't have recognized him."

This does not mean that women are without sexual or romantic partners during these years, however. Some women continue to follow a "hook up" pattern that was established in college. They go out to clubs and bars and have casual sex "for fun." Some of the 30-something women I interviewed describe the years right after college as their "wild" time. More commonly, however, they report two or three relationships of varying duration and seriousness in the immediate post-college years. Some form living-together partnerships. As noted previously, the majority of young women today will live with a boyfriend, either the man they eventually marry or another intimate partner, before they marry.

Cohabiting partnerships represent a distinctive new feature of the early adult life course. For many young adults, cohabitation provides a transitional kind of union, somewhere between casual dating relationships and marriage. Women enter cohabiting partnerships for a variety of reasons, including the economies of time and money, the desire for sex, intimacy, and partnership rolled into one, and the need to get to know more about the habits, character, and compatibility of a romantic partner. Indeed, cohabitation fulfills some of the same purposes as traditional courtship. Women often have sex with their boyfriend before they get to know him well as a human being. Consequently, for them, cohabitation provides a way to observe and learn about their partner by sharing a roof as well as a bed.

At the same time that cohabitation offers some of the features of courtship and marriage, it permits a high degree of separateness and independence. For both men and women, the lower level of commitment can be an advantage during the time of life when they want to be free to pursue opportunities in work or schooling. They can make decisions about their next step in life without an obligation to coordinate their plans with their living-together partner. And, of course, they are free to move on at any time.

This high turnover, low-commitment pattern in early adult love relationships resembles patterns of early career development. Indeed, in the years following college, the pursuit of love is nearly identical to the pursuit of work. Like early work experiences, romantic relationships tend to be instructive, memorable, but short-term arrangements. When some women talk about their 20-something relationships, they seem to be describing entry-level jobs. They characterize their romances as part of a process of learning and self-discovery rather than part of a search for a lifelong mate. Even the experience of being dumped, like getting fired or downsized, women say, can be a learning opportunity that helps them to grow and to learn more about what they truly need and want in a mate.

But there is a down side to this new pattern in early adult intimate relationships. Whether it's casual dating or cohabitation, the cycle of low-commitment relationships eventually begins to exact a toll. Getting in and out of relationships consumes emotional energy and substantial investments of time. After several years of dating, many single women begin to experience what can only be described as relationships fatigue. They get tired of going out to bars and clubs. It's not as much fun as it used to be. And they begin to "age out" of the club scene. The crowd is full of 20-something men who are just looking for a good time and a chance to get laid and 20-something women who are out for the same thing. "There's no quicker way to feel ugly than the club scene," one 31-year-old lawyer says. "It seems like younger men and women are dictating the rules of the dating game, and these rules (or lack of them) terrify me," another single woman tells me. "It's a lot easier to be a sexual adventuress when your eggs aren't nearing their expiration date."

Relationships fatigue can also descend in the aftermath of a breakup. Ending a relationship saps energy and desire, of course, but it's not only the breakup that takes a toll. It's the emotional recovery time. Getting over a relationship takes twice the time of the relationship itself, according to many women who have been through it. Women describe their post-breakup period like a flu bug that is hard to shake: they feel "listless," "confused," "zombielike." Weariness settles into the brain as well as the bones. The very thought of "putting yourself out there" is exhausting. A good book and a warm bath can seem more enticing and pleasurable than another night out at a club. Like discouraged workers, some women decide to drop out of the mating market for a while.

In addition, the relationships boom-and-bust cycle can leave a residue of mistrust and hurt that makes some women wary of future relationships. This emotional residue is like plaque on teeth: it builds up, hardens, and is often tough to get rid of without the help of a specialist. In many cities, relationships-weary professional women are lining up at therapists' offices to figure out what's gone wrong in their love lives, and more than a few therapists have built a thriving practice devoted to scraping off the emotional plaque accumulated over a succession of romantic failures and disappointments.[4]

Over time, moreover, the pursuit of love also faces competition from work. By the time ambitious single women reach their late 20s, their career investments are beginning to pay off. The years of schooling, interning, temping, and career-building have led to absorbing, high-paying positions with heavy time and travel commitments. Leila, a Stanford graduate and lawyer, works as a Title IX compliance athletic director for a Southwestern college. Her work responsibilities consume almost all her time. In the morning, she gets up and goes to the gym to work out and then to her office. She usually has a game to attend after work, so she heads back to the gym. "I'm not home until after 9:30 or 10:00 P.M., and if the game is a doubleheader, it's even later. I also take a class one night a week." On weekends, Leila spends Friday night "doing something with my family"; attends a game on Saturday afternoon and another one that night; and devotes Sunday to church and getting ready for the week ahead.

There are also the "roller bag" women. Clarissa, a marketing director for a fast-growing, fast-paced consulting group in Washington, spends three or four days a week, three weeks out of every month, on the road and in the air. When she gets home at the end of a travel week, she barely has time to do laundry, shopping, and bill-paying before she has to get ready for another 5:00 A.M. wake up and another trek back to Reagan National. Patricia's work as a business consultant for one of the Big Eight accounting firms puts her on the road about 75 percent of the time. "I travel so much because I'm driven by the best projects," she explains. "And I'm a workaholic and perfectionist, so I don't follow the 80/20 rule that says when the job is 80 percent done, you should move on."

Sometimes, careers make it necessary to sustain long-distance relationships. Jacqui, 32, had a long-distance relationship with another lawyer in her firm. He was smart, exciting, and had a "superspark," and the intensity and exhilaration of their romance propelled things forward at a very fast rate. After a year of dating they lived together, but then he left to begin an MBA in another city. They commuted from their respective East Coast cities for weekends, and after his graduation they were married. However, once married, Jacqui realized how incompatible they were. The momentum and excitement of their romance, along with the two years of living apart, had prevented them from recognizing, much less acknowledging, serious differences. Though both were highly successful in their careers, he was far more career-primary than she was. She had supported his career ambitions and pursuit of another professional degree, but she hadn't realized how driven he was until they were married. His career mania wasn't so noticeable or problematic when they lived in separate cities; but once they were married, Jacqui discovered its practical implications: "I'd sleep alone on nine out of ten nights, and on the tenth night, he would be grouchy."

Despite the time pressures of work, however, professional single women have full social lives. Their calendars are crowded with events, activities, and appointments: they fund raise, volunteer, play on intramural sports teams, attend Bible studies, go to book clubs and concerts, campaign for political candidates or causes, spend time with mothers and sisters, vacation with friends, and go out on occasional "girls nights out." Many own their own condos or houses, so they are busy building their nests at the same time as they are building their careers. Indeed, the rate of homeownership in female one-person households has risen from the early 1980s to the present. In 1982, for example, the rate was slightly more than 35 percent for women ages 35 to 39; by 2000, it had risen to nearly 45 percent.[5] After women acquire real estate, they find themselves investing their weekend time at furniture showrooms, linen sales, gardening centers, antique stores, and country auctions rather than at clubs or social events. Houses are easier to repair, refurbish, and love than many men.

These activities take time and energy away from dating. Moreover, compared to dating, they often offer more reliable returns on the investment. In Wall Street terms, friendship is a bond, but a romantic relationship is a speculative stock. A night out with the girls has reliable satisfactions and pay-offs whereas a night out with a blind date can be a total loss. "I now go to parties to meet interesting women," a straight Manhattanite tells me. But it's not simply time pressures that contribute to women's romantic discontents. It is also the growing sense—sometimes imposed by others—that they've been heedless of time. These young women have been planners and time managers ever since they were young, but the timing of marriage was not something that was a pressing concern. It was one of those things that happened when the time was right. "I'm truly surprised that I am still single," a 28-year-old sales executive tells me. "And people keep asking me why. I know that they mean it in a flattering way, that I'm attractive and intelligent and a 'good catch,' but it still makes me feel like I've missed some kind of deadline." "I'm 28, well-educated, own my own business, and have a very fun, happy life," a first-time personal ad placer writes, "but it seems that everybody got married while I was busy!"

A SHIFT IN ROMANTIC PRIORITIES

SOMETIME AFTER THEIR MID-20S, women say that they enter a new stage in their dating careers. They shift from hooking up and casual dating to more serious searching for a soul mate. "Before my 28th birthday hit," says Elizabeth West, the heroine in *The Cigarette Girl*, a 1999 novel about one single woman's dating discontents, "I was perfectly happy to live my single life. Work. Work out. And sex. That's all I needed."[6] But beyond 28, Elizabeth began to see things differently. ". . . My heart was still with the wild girls yet there was a part of me . . . call it female instinct or millions of years of DNA memory, that felt a tug toward—if not yet motherhood—some kind of couplehood."[7]

It's hard to predict exactly when this shift in romantic priorities will occur. For some women, like Christina, it comes around age 30. For others, it happens much later. "Thirty-nine was such a miserable year for men," one just-turned-40 Bay Area professional confesses. "I never felt much of an urge to actually get married and have kids. I just assumed that by 40, though, I would have achieved those things." But it's not always a milestone birthday that triggers the shift in women's priorities. Sometimes it's a significant event. It could be an invitation to the wedding of an ex-boyfriend who still figures in one's "maybe-someday-we'll-get-back-together" fantasies. Or it could be the unexpected pang over the purchase of a Baby Gap outfit for a girlfriend's new baby. Or a stab of jealousy over a younger sister's engagement. Or the loss of a job. Or a major breakup. Or the illness or death of a parent. Or, after September 11, the new awareness of the fragility of life and its sometimes sudden and tragic end.

Whenever the moment dawns, women begin to obsess over things that barely used to reach the level of their conscious awareness. Younger women, for one thing. Sometime in the late '90s, Christina says, she began to notice that the 20-something women at work were wearing tighter, sluttier clothes than she would ever consider wearing herself. It's not that she felt insecure about her own body; she worked out, looked good, and could compete with younger women in the buffed body department. But she had standards. Sadly, she observes, many single men didn't share her standards. They actually seemed to like these younger, sexually exhibitionist women. Sarah, 27, a marketing director for an international strategic consulting firm, detects another pattern. The family-oriented single men in her church are getting engaged to younger women who are not as committed to serious careers or not as far along in their careers as she is. Another young woman tells me, "We're in a war of 20 somethings vs. 30 somethings."

If younger women are a reminder of the passage of time, so too are the little signs of aging. Why do I have bags under my eyes after eight hours sleep? Where did that little blue vein burst come from? Should I try Botox? City magazines catering to single professionals are full of advertisements for laser surgery, botox injections, breast augmentation, spider and varicose vein treatment, or "wellness surgery," as it is called in the trade. These are procedures ideally positioned to appeal to younger women who are not yet ready for the full face and neck lift but are able to spend some money for a tuck here, a laser there, a tightening everywhere. Indeed, the fastest growing segment of the cosmetic surgery market is women in their 20s and 30s, and for reasons that go beyond personal vanity. There is competition in the mating market. According to one recent study, both young men and young women today place a much higher value on physical attractiveness and sexiness in a mate than in years past.[8] Perhaps for this reason, the ads for cosmetic surgical services appear in close proximity to ads for dating services.

Most insistently, there are anxieties over aging eggs. If some hyper-careerist baby boom women "forgot" to have babies, as the famous cartoon once suggested, today's young single women are well aware of the ticking of their biological clock. They have obsessively gone through the calculations of the time they have left—what some women describe to me as "doing the math." Christina had already decided that she had to have her first child by age 39. Backcounting from that deadline, she figured that she had six or seven years to find a prospective husband. This gave her plenty of time to meet her baby deadline as long as she didn't waste any of it on going-nowhere relationships. Of course, if she hadn't found Mr. Right by her late 30s, she could extend her deadline by several years. Thanks to the wizardry of the pharmaceutical industry, fertility drugs could put time on the baby clock.

But even with additional time afforded by fertility drugs, if she waited too long she faced the increased likelihood of infertility, the risks of multiple births, or other complications of pregnancy. True, Christina said, she could adopt a child on her own. But single motherhood was her default plan, and she was not a default plan kind of girl. "I think it's kind of ironic," another woman in the same situation tells me. "We spend our teens and 20s worrying about not getting pregnant so that we can spend our 30s and 40s worrying about getting pregnant."

Christina knows that she can be a single career woman with a baby, if she chooses. And if and when she chooses, she can achieve that goal on her own. Two out of three—a baby and a job—are within her control. However, she does not see that as the most desirable option. She wants a husband before she has a child, and as a progressive woman, she expects her future partner to share fully in household and childrearing responsibilities.

For Christina, therefore, the challenge is to find the right man at the right time. Now that she has reached the time that is right for her, she faces the challenge of finding a man who is ready to marry and who shares her goals for a family. This means that she has to be more aware of time. During most of her 20s, she assumed that there was plenty of time to find a life partner. What's more, she expected that one of her relationships would work out and lead to marriage. It was supposed to happen without much conscious effort. However, at 31, she realizes that she has a limited time to find a husband, if she is to achieve her goal of marriage and children. And each year is valuable. She can't afford to waste her time in another relationship with Mr. Not Ready.

Also, Christina realizes that it is more difficult than it once was to find a man who is available and suitable for marriage. Many of the men she might have considered husband material are already someone else's husband. Other suitable men are unavailable because they are already partnered up. Among the available men, many are unsuitable. Some remain stuck in a chronic state of romantic irresolution, a bunch of Mr. Not Readys who are on the verge of turning into Mr. Never Readys. Other unsuitables in the mating pool include an odd assortment of "toss-them-back-in" guys: married men who want to have a girlfriend on the side; divorced men who still aren't over their ex; older never-married men who are suspect because they have never been married. (Are they gay? Are they sexually weird? Are they slackers? Are they still in love with Mom?)

Christina's challenge is to find one available and suitable man who shares her goals for marriage and family and is ready to commit to these responsibilities. But she has no easy way or reliable method to differentiate the marriage-ready men from those who are not likely to be interested in or ready for marriage. Trial and error seems to be the only possible approach, but too many trials will prolong the search and too many errors will make it more painful and difficult.

CHAPTER II

THE "NO GOOD MEN" PLAINT

IF ANYTHING HAS COME TO REPRESENT the romantic plight of the new single woman, it is the familiar lament—"There are no good men left." I first heard this sentiment about a decade ago when I was attending a conference on social trends. One of the speakers, a distinguished sociology professor, noted that the marriage rate has declined in recent decades. The marriage rate is the number of marriages per 1000 unmarried women, 15 and over, per year. The marriage rate is not necessarily a measure of women's eventual marriage prospects, but many women take it to be. So the professor's observation elicited an annoyed reaction from some of the women in the room. A 30ish female reporter shot back: "Why should we drive ourselves crazy about getting married? We work hard to get ahead in our careers and by the time we are ready to get married, most of the good men are already taken."

Today, the "no good men" notion is part of the dating lore that women endlessly discuss. It is a recurrent theme in HBO's *Sex and the City* and its knockoffs and in the many novels devoted to the lives and loves of today's single women. The 32-year-old heroine of Tama Janowitz's *A Certain Age* compares her frustrating search for a boyfriend to a losing game of musical chairs: "Ninety-nine percent of them were taken, and she couldn't see where the empty ones were positioned. Besides, if there were any empty chairs left, they were empty for a reason—broken legs, ugly styles, cheap imitations."[1] Even the greeting card industry has picked up on this plaint: at my local CVS, I find greeting cards with the message "Why are men like parking spaces? All the good ones are taken."

THE PLAINT BY THE NUMBERS

THERE HAVE BEEN TWO PRINCIPAL SOURCES for the "no good men" plaint.[2] One is a widely circulated set of sociological projections of women's chances for marriage. The other is a new genre of popular fiction. Let's consider the sociological version first. Perhaps the biggest contributor to the persistent view that marriage-minded women will be unable to marry because there aren't enough good men for them has been the continuing influence of a 1986 cover story in *Newsweek*. Entitled "Too Late for Prince Charming," the article heralded a marriage crunch for college-educated women. The number of single women with college degrees, it said, greatly exceeded the number of available peer men. At the age of 35, it said, a never-married college-educated woman had only a 5 percent chance of ever marrying. At 40, it famously predicted, such a woman's chances of finding a husband were worse than her chances of getting attacked by terrorists.[3]

In its story, the magazine took pains to note how tentative and narrow these predictions were. They were merely projections, it said, and they applied only to women who were in the older half of the baby boom. (Lately, these women have been turning 50.) It also cautioned readers to view the numbers with a grain of salt, because they were based on an unpublished academic study that had not yet been scrutinized by other social scientists in the field. But many readers failed to heed these cautions and took the dire projections at face value.

Shortly after the *Newsweek* story appeared, a demographer at the Census Bureau attempted the same projections but used a different statistical method. The resulting estimates were substantially higher than those made in the study reported by *Newsweek*. At age 35, according to the Census study, a never-married college-educated woman had as much as a 41 percent chance of getting married. These odds are eight times better than the odds cited in the *Newsweek* story. But this prediction wasn't featured on the cover of a national newsmagazine. Consequently, it didn't exert nearly as much public impact as the *Newsweek* numbers, and so it couldn't serve as a truly effective challenge to them.[4]

Since the *Newsweek* story appeared, its glum forecast has continued to reverberate through successive waves of young college-educated women. Its predictions were based on data that is now 18 years old. They applied to women born in the early 1950s. And they were quickly contested by a much different set of projections. Nevertheless, there are women in their 20s and 30s today who believe the predictions apply to them.

Recently, two sociologists at Princeton have come up with a new updated set of projections. Their projections, published in *The American Sociological Review* in 2001, aren't based on single college women who are in their 20s and 30s today, but neither are they based on women who are in their 50s. Notably, they are radically different from the *Newsweek* numbers. For never-married white college-educated women who were ages 30 through 34 in the mid-1990s, these estimates suggest, the chances for marriage could be as high as 97 percent.[5]

The researchers conclude: "we predict that marriage levels will be highest for those women who are, in theory, most able to live well alone—the most highly educated."

The fact is, we can never know for sure what the likelihood of future marriage is for women who are single today. Any attempt to establish this likelihood can only be a prediction based on a set of assumptions about marrying behavior of women in the past. And, of course, demographic predictions can turn out to be wrong. Nevertheless, there are intriguing reasons why the projections made by the Princeton study may be on target. They have to do with the changes in the historical pattern in the timing of marriage.

For decades, women typically married in their late teens or early 20s. As a result, the overwhelming majority of first marriages by women were concentrated within a narrow age range. If a woman hadn't married by the time she'd gone beyond the high end of that age range, there was at least a statistically based reason to think that she might never marry at all. Thus, for those women, marriage delayed might well have proven to be marriage denied.

In recent years, however, the ages of the first marriages by college-educated women have not been as tightly bunched within a narrow range. Their ages of entry into marriage have been spreading out across a wider age spectrum. And almost all of this spreading has moved in a single direction: toward older ages. Thus, there has been a weakening in the historical pattern. Delays in the age of first marriage are no longer as likely to lead to denial of marriage. Today, even if women aren't married by 25, or 35, they may still get married.

More to the point, according to the Princeton researchers, the chances that an educated woman will marry at a relatively older age appear to be better than they were for college women in the past. In other words, a Gloria Steinem effect may be developing, whereby some women marry for the first time at an age that is significantly later than what used to fall within the normal range—though perhaps not as late as it was for Steinem herself, who married for the first time at 66.

Just as the "delayed equals denied" pattern has weakened, so has the pattern of women marrying men who are older than they are. Of currently married women, 48 percent of those who married in the 1970s and 1980s were the same age or older than their husbands. This is true of just 38 percent of women who married in the years 1945 through 1964.[6]

THE PLAINT BY THE BOOK

IN ADDITION TO THE SOCIOLOGICAL version of the plaint, there is its literary version. It can be found in the new genre of popular fiction which some have characterized as Chick Lit. Each of two successive generations of college-educated women can point to a signature literature that marks its coming of age. For young women in the '60s and '70s, it was a literature of politics, and particularly feminist politics. Many of the bestselling books of the time took aim against the forces in society that limited women's freedom and opportunities. These were works of argument, dissent, and feminist protest. From Betty Friedan's *The Feminine Mystique* to Gloria Steinem's *Ms.* magazine to Susan Brownmiller's *Against Our Will,* this literature called for political action against institutionalized forms of injustice, discrimination, and violence against women.

Today, the appeal of this literature of liberation has faded. Young women aren't reading their mothers' manifestos. Instead, they are immersed in Chick Lit. Its authors come from a different world than the women who created the Lib Lit of the earlier generation. Unlike the feminist advocates and academics of the '60s and '70s, they didn't cut their teeth in consciousness-raising groups and graduate seminars, but in the competitive ranks of the popular media, where they work as sex and relationships columnists, scriptwriters, fashion editors, and journalists on the entertainment and celebrity beats. The tone and temper of Chick Lit are also different. Chick Lit authors don't write with gravitas, and there is little political or moral earnestness in their books. Instead, their works are full of oneliners, quips, jokes, put-downs, put-ons, comebacks, and wisecracks. A playful literature has replaced a polemical one. But the most culturally revealing and distinctive feature of this new genre is its subject matter. It is obsessively devoted to one theme: smart young women's frustrations with men and dating relationships.

In its view of men, Chick Lit is a fascinating departure from Lib Lit. For nearly half a century, women have publicly expressed their anger at men. But today's grievance is different from the political outrage that animated baby boom women. Sixties feminists viewed men as the beneficiaries of male privilege. Thus, they took a stand against the UberMale, a prototypical Male Chauvinist who embodied patriarchy and institutional sexism. He was the Hardhat who wolf-whistled at women on the street. He was the Campus Radical who ordered his female comrades to go make the coffee. He was the Boss who expected his female employees to act like office wives. This anger could be expressed politically. It gave rise to marches, bra-burnings, picketings, and demonstrations. Chick Lit views men less as the target for political outrage than as the source of chronic romantic disappointment. It views men in their private and indeed intimate roles. What's in its foreground isn't men as a gender or an oppressor class. It's the man in your life, or the man who just got out of your life, or the man who is missing from your life. Yesterday's Hardhat and Campus Radical and Boss have been replaced by today's Mr. Cheater and Mr. Not Ready. In Chick Lit, the personal isn't political. It's personal.

In the new literature, there is also a different emotional atmos-phere—a complicated stew of anger, regret, and rue. Part of it is a mistrust of men, the emotional residue of bad breakups. Part of it is a simmering resentment over the way one particular man broke it off. Part of it is relationships fatigue, a discouragement and weariness with the dating game itself. And some of the anger is turned inward, as a self-reproach for one's own misjudgments. It asks not only "How Could He Do This to Me?," but also, "How Could I Let Him Do This to Me?"

One of the first writers to limn the literary version of the "no-good-men" theme was Pam Houston, whose bestselling collection of short stories, *Cowboys Are My Weakness* (1992), was followed by a similarly themed volume of stories, *Waltzing the Cat*, in 1998. Houston's stories revolve around the extreme outdoor adventures of independent 30-something women who meet up with one feckless, selfish, untrustworthy guy after another. The typical Houston hero-ine is chronically attracted to, and repeatedly dumped by, cowboys, mechanics, carpenters, wilderness guides, and other men's men who abandon her for their solitary Marlboro Man pursuits or for the next woman they meet on the trail. The linked stories in *Waltzing the Cat* follow wilderness photographer Lucille O'Rourke as she hikes, climbs, or rafts from one dangerous locale to another. Lucy is as accomplished in the wilds as any guy; she can take on the Colorado rapids and the Amazonian jungles, face down grizzlies, and talk bat-ting averages. Her adventures are filled with physical highs, moments when she performs feats of courage, strength, and endurance, and romantic lows, moments when she loses her balance and equilibrium over a man. As Lucy scales mountains and shoots class-six rapids, she sinks into ever more depressing relationships with unworthy or unsuitable men. Her problem isn't with the quan-tity of men; she works in a man's world where there is a glut of unmarried guys who share her passion for adventure. Her problem is the quality of the men she finds. Lucy's "cowboys" are wild and fear-less in their macho pursuits, but when it comes to loving a woman, they turn timid and irresolute. Her cowboy can't venture anything so brave or daring as commitment to one woman. He likes to put a lot of wide-open space between him and his little lady; the long-distance relationship—separate lives with sex (or cybersex) sandwiched in between—is the kind of relationship that these cowboys like best. Unlike the classic hero of the West, not all of Houston's guys are the strong, silent type. Some are emotionally screwed up and eager to talk about it. Even worse, these New Age cowboys exploit their emotional weakness by turning it into a form of intimacy: "You bring up the word 'monogamy.' He'll tell you how badly hurt he was by your predecessor. He'll say he's scared and confused."[7]

One of the long-distance boyfriends who cycles in and out of Lucy's life is Carter, a movie location scout with a fiancée in L.A. Lucy and Carter enjoy a "virtual relationship" via phone and answering machine; he's a traveling man and his layovers at Lucy's place are hurried and brief. When he favors Lucy with his presence, they backpack, sail, and raft together before he takes off again for a new destination. But these stolen moments are layovers without lays: they sleep together (Carter in a T-shirt with no bottoms), but they don't have sex. When Lucy snuggles closer to him in bed, he pulls away. Lucy has another boyfriend, a crazy drunk named Erik: he's tender, sweet, and good with power tools. He fixes her plumbing and wiring and the tilted foundation of her house. But after they've gotten romantic, he confesses that his own power tool is out of commission. For the last two years, his anti-depressants have left him impotent.

What is even more painful is the casual cruelty with which Houston's cowboys take their leave. Breakups are a predictable part of relationships. Carter, the peripatetic movie locations scout, stops by to take Lucy on a hiking trip and then breaks up with her on the trail when she complains about the lack of sex in their relationship. They hike in silence for the next two days, while Carter pauses every now and then to scribble notes on a piece of paper. Later, back at the trailhead, the paper falls out of Carter's pocket and Lucy has a chance to pick it up and read it. The piece of paper contains a list of her physical features that Carter finds unappealing: "1. Too broad through the shoulders; 2. Upper lip too thin; 3. Unappealing waist-to-hip ratio . . ." and on and on.[8] In another story, Lucy gets dumped as she rushes to her boyfriend in Michigan after returning from a trip down the Amazon. Expecting to be swept into his arms, she is instead greeted with a breakup speech: "'We need to have a little talk first,' he said, patting my hand like I was an old person. 'I'm sorry, Lucy, but I've met someone new. It feels really healthy so far.'"[9] It's not only the hand patting that makes a reader wince, but also the staggering egocentricity of a man who imagines that his just-dumped, jet-lagged girlfriend would share his happiness over a "healthy" new relationship.

Houston's stories offer a portrait gallery of men behaving badly, but upon closer inspection, her gallery contains multiple images of just one guy. Despite the variations in jobs, names, and hair color, Houston's cowboys are as interchangeable as subway tokens. In her lexicon, "cowboy" is just another name for all emotionally unavailable men. In the Reading Group Guide to the paperback edition of *Cowboys Are My Weakness*, Houston writes, "What really surprised me was how universal my characters' situations turned out to be. I got letters from women all over the country: firemen are my weakness, stockbrokers are my weakness, the list was as long as there are professions. Apparently, the type of man I was writing about is not region- or profession-specific."[10]

Though Houston establishes the "no good men" theme, other writers add new elements to her portrait. A successor batch of Chick Lit books takes up the same subject but with some important differences. Houston's stories are bleak; Chick Lit is light and spoofy. Dating betrayals, dumpings, and disappointments are played for laughs. The authors make fun of men. They make fun of sex. They make fun of women. They make fun of themselves. The blurbs for these books reflect the new comic spirit: "acerbically funny," "hilarious," "sparkling with wit," "a hoot," "amusingly high- spirited." (One blurb praised a novel for having so many sentences worth underlining.)

Besides the change in tone, there is a shift in locale. In Chick Lit novels, the 30-something heroine moves from West to East, from the glow of the campfire to the city lights of New York and London. As the Chick Lit heroines migrate eastward, the western wilderness becomes the urban jungle, and Lucy morphs into several New York Janes, including Jane Goodall, the character in Laura Zigman's *Animal Husbandry* (1998), Jane Rosenal in Melissa Bank's *The Girls' Guide to Hunting and Fishing* (1999), and a new Jane in a Harlequin series that begins with *See Jane Date* (2001).

In these novels of romantic dejection and rejection, the single women heroines are also dumped, humiliated, deceived, betrayed by men, but unlike Houston's Lucy, they no longer ache with regret or cringe with remorse. Instead, they retaliate with one-liners, quips, jokes, and comic shtick about men and their inadequacies. Comedy is their preferred form of aggression. For characters in the novels, writing is the best revenge. As one observes, "It's the ultimate revenge fantasy. You get rich and famous writing about something you're already obsessed with." In *Run Catch Kiss*, the fictional heroine takes revenge on the disgusting men she dates by literally kissing and telling, exposing their weird sexual predilections in the sex column she writes.[11]

Some characters echo Houston's universal cowboy theme. In Candace Bushnell's *Sex and the City*, Charlotte, the English journalist, explains why she won't date men who are ordinary looking: "I've gone out with some of those guys—the ones who are short, fat, and ugly—and it doesn't make any difference. They're just as unappreciative and self-centered as the good looking ones."[12] In other books, women take revenge on men by treating them as casually and indiscriminately as they themselves are treated by men.

The Chick Lit heroines also make a point of showing how little emotional investment they put into a relationship by identifying men by number rather than name, since some are anonymous and others are so easily forgotten. Lucinda Rosenfeld's novel, *What She Saw*, is organized in a chapter-by-chapter list of serial boyfriends, including one chapter devoted to "Anonymous 1–4." Another character in Rosenfeld's novel keeps track of her sex partners by their geographic location: "If she'd screwed them in the parking lot of a Grateful Dead show, she'd give them code names like 'Deadhead One,' 'Deadhead Two,' 'Deadhead Three.'"[13]

Other novels pay homage to fashionable theories of evolutionary psychology. According to the popular version of these theories, men are male animals, with the same lust for variety, youth, beauty, and big breasts as a chimp, gorilla, or any other male beast. Laura Zigman's 1998 bestseller, *Animal Husbandry*, is a spoofy case study in what the heroine calls the Old Cow/New Cow theory of mating. After her boyfriend dumps her, the heroine, Jane Goodall, turns to animal research to figure out why men flee. She invents a mating theory based on the observation that a bull will ditch an old cow as soon as a new cow appears, and then gets a job writing about the theory as a pseudonymous science columnist for a men's magazine.[14] In this novel, as in others, falling in love and mating (life as a New Cow) is mere prologue. It's getting dumped (life as an Old Cow) that constitutes the main interest and action in the story.

Whatever the species, the point is that male mating behavior is predictable: he seeks variety and flees from commitment. The novels document the routine symptoms of an impending dumping: he hides behind his answering machine, shows up late, fails to return repeated messages, makes excuses for not meeting friends or family, backpedals after you bring up the question of "where is this relationship going?," makes frequent plans that leave you out, remains semi-attached to an old girlfriend. And his breakup speeches are just as predictable and scripted as his retreat. Accordingly, you know it's over when he says (pick one): (a) "This week is going to be terrible. I'm completely swamped." (b) "I think maybe we should cool things for a while." (c) "A little voice tells me something isn't right." (d) "I've been doing a lot of thinking lately." The theme of sexual humiliation, never far from the surface in much of this literature, erupts full force in Lucinda Rosenfeld's novel, *What She Saw* (2000). After too many desperation lays, the protagonist Phoebe Fine is sexually numb and emotionally shut-down. She can't feel intimacy with anyone. In fact, the sweeter the guy, the more she despises him: "Phoebe could walk in on her perfectly nice boyfriend pissing in the bathroom and the sight of him standing over the pot doing what was, after all, only natural, would disgust her beyond reason."[15]

Critics have been harshly dismissive of much of this literature, deriding it as formula fiction for young women still emotionally stuck in junior high. And if these works are judged on the basis of artistry or originality alone, the critics have a point. For the most part, the novels are slight entertainments, and after you've gotten a laugh or two out of the sitcomish characters, you aren't even that entertained. Moreover, because some of the women heroines are so emotionally needy, their sex lives so depressing and unromantic, it is hard to feel any sympathy or interest in them. And the farcical spine of Chick Lit is not so much a sign of resilience as a defense against the inevitability of hurt, humiliation and heartbreak.

It would be a mistake to read Chick Lit as a documentary record of the love lives of actual single women or as a description of their actual mating prospects. What makes this fiction notable is not its literary artistry or documentary accuracy but its popular appeal to a reading audience of young, educated single women. There is something in Chick Lit's portrait of dating and mating that jibes with many single women's own experience. If not sociologically true, Chick Lit nonetheless captures an emotional truth about women's dissatisfactions with men and the contemporary dating scene.

There is yet another reason to pay attention to Chick Lit. Historically, there is a relationship between the rise of popular romantic literature and the upheaval in the system of courtship itself. On at least two earlier occasions in Western society, art and life came together in a new genre. The *Roman de la Rose*, the great poem of chivalric love, appeared in medieval France at a time when feudal society was undergoing massive changes that presaged the end of feudalism itself. In order to prevent the fragmentation of family property and power, noble families transmitted their wealth to the oldest sons, who were then able to marry. However, this practice left a glut of dispossessed, unmarriageable young men who could not attain the status of adult males until they could marry a woman with a substantial dowry. In the meantime, these *juvenes*, as they were called, wandered around the court with nothing much to do but engage in fantasies of sexual conquest and seduction. Out of this socially combustible situation emerged a literature aimed at instructing young men in the art of romance and in the romantic quest of a fair and unattainable married lady. The *Roman de la Rose* transformed a jobless group of young single men into the proverbial knights in shining armor.

Likewise, the eighteenth-century novel arose at a time when English society was becoming more fluid, individualistic, and market-oriented, changing the traditional patterns of home manufacturing and creating a glut of unmarried women who could not stay at home and work but had to work for wages outside the home. Young, unmarried women from poor families took jobs as maids, cooks, and nannies. Those above the ranks of the serving classes searched for respectable employment as governesses, but their opportunities for paid work befitting their social station were severely limited. As long as they stayed unmarried, many were forced to remain burdensome dependents within the family household, living off the oftentimes meager and grudging charity of their kin.

Such changing conditions in the lives of young women placed a new premium on marriage, for marriage was increasingly viewed as the principal route out of wage slavery or genteel poverty. However, at the same time, these changes created new risks and uncertainties for the not-yet married. Out of this social tumult emerged the novel, aimed at a growing audience of women readers and featuring an estimable young woman's search for a rich husband. The novel transformed an economically vulnerable population of young single women into the proverbial romantic heroine.

Chick Lit has appeared at a similar moment of social change. It testifies to an upheaval in the patterns of love and work in women's lives. This upheaval doesn't make it less likely that a marriage-minded, college-educated single woman of today will ultimately marry. But it can exert a powerful effect on her efforts to find the right man at the right time. It can make her attempts at finding a life partner more confusing, prolonged, and difficult. It won't necessarily turn her search into a failure. But it can make it an ordeal.

THE ODDS ARE GOOD BUT THE GOODS ARE ODD

SUSAN, 29, IS AN ENTREPRENEUR. Like Christina, she has reached the time in her life when she is seriously thinking about marriage and children. The outdated projections in *Newsweek* and the hyperbolic sketches in Chick Lit don't speak to the letter of her problem—she has finished an MBA and is out in the world and hasn't come upon dispositive evidence of an absolute shortage of men who are available and suitable for marriage—but they fit its spirit. What is hard for her is finding these men. They are out there, but where do you look for them? How do you meet them? Where are the readymade social occasions to do so? Given her busy professional schedule, how does she free up the time and opportunity to do the looking? And what are the ways for her to distinguish the men who are ready for marriage from those who will prefer less committed partnerships?

Susan is one of the most delightful young women I interviewed in the course of my research. She is lively and engaging with a quick wit and a natural leader's gift for reaching out to people. She grew up in a small town in the South with parents who were the first children in their respective families to get college degrees and then go on to get advanced degrees. They instilled a deep belief in the importance of education as something "no one can take away from you." From an early age, Susan knew that she was going to try to exceed her parents' educational achievements, and they encouraged that ambition, promising that money would never be an obstacle for her or her sister's educational pursuits. Her father switched from the nonprofit sector to the corporate sector and the family moved to a metropolitan area where Susan attended an inner city magnet school, more culturally diverse than the university she later attended, and rich in AP courses, language immersion classes, and opportunities to attend classes at the nearby college. She was a good student, but her greatest strength was as a student leader. She moved up in the ranks of student government and landed on the staff of the national leadership camp.

At the elite university she attended, she continued to stand out as a leader. She was involved in campus activities and, in her senior year, was voted Head Resident in a senior honors dorm whose members were selected from the academic, athletic, and altruistic superstars on campus. Susan's job was to build a sense of community among this elite group, the busiest of the busy, the most talented of the talented.

At her coed university, Susan had convenient access to a geographically localized pool of peer men who were closely matched to peer women on the basis of age, marital status, and educational attainment. Nearly every undergraduate male was a never-married, high-achieving high school graduate between the ages of 18 and 23. What's more, her university offered many social opportunities to get to know her male peers. It had a strong Greek system, but more than that, it had a wealth of campus activities and organizations, each with its own calendar of social activities. And Susan was involved in many of these campus activities. However, she notes, her university was not a "dating" school. "You might get a date to go to a formal but even then," she says, "you were looking for a friend to take you." People "hooked up," but "hooking up" did not always mean casual sex. Sometimes, it meant something more innocent and comradely: people "hooked up" just for the purpose of hanging out with someone for a night or having a partner at a party, she explains. Among the groups of close friends who hung out together, there were usually a few couples who were practically married, but most of the people in her crowd were more closely attached to the friendship group than to a romantic partner.

More to the point, though, Susan wasn't ready to take advantage of her easy access to a large pool of marriage-eligible peer men, because at that stage in her life, she wasn't ready to get married. Nor were most of the men in her college crowd. Thus, for her, and others like her, the years in the college mating pool no longer coincide with what they regard as their prime time to find someone to marry.

Meanwhile, Susan was moving ahead in her early career development. She spent her college summers in progressively responsible internships, and, during her senior year, she was courted by several major corporations that cruise the colleges for undergraduate leaders. Susan took a job with a Big Eight accounting firm. During her first two years on this job, "I put stakes in the ground. I attended Bible study on Monday nights, met friends for dinner one night a week, lived in a house with other women in a young singles neighborhood. I had plenty of socializing. I didn't have to search for it."

Then the firm sent her on the road, and her social life almost vanished. She found herself working so much that she couldn't plan anything social, lest a last-minute work assignment force her to cancel. And if it then turned out that she didn't have to work on a weekend, she was left without any social plans, and with little but work to fill the time. After two years on the road, she was ready to move on.

By the age of 26, Susan had decided she couldn't wait much longer if she wanted to accomplish her long-standing goal of getting an MBA. "It was something I always wanted to do, and I started to do the math. I would be 29 when I got out, and I would need to work at least two years after to get the value of the degree. I would be 32 before I could think about getting married and having kids. So I couldn't put it off any longer."

She got into an elite business school and thrived. At this time in her life, she wasn't as indifferent to finding a man to marry as she had been during her undergraduate years. In addition to being close to the prime time for marrying, she also had what looked to be a prime pool of graduate school men who were similarly matched by education and age. Indeed, in her business school class, men vastly outnumbered women. In a class of 240, there were 190 men and 50 women. Of the 190 men, half were married. That left 95 singles, still a favorable male to female ratio. Of those 95 men, however, about 50 were currently in committed relationships. That left 45 men who were single and available for a smaller number of available women of similar education and age. (Some of the 50 women in the class were married or partnered as well, so the ratio was advantageous for the women who were still unpartnered.)

On paper, the odds clearly favored the women. In the flesh, however, it was a different story. "There's a reason why those men are left in the pool," says Susan. "They are either drinking themselves silly on the weekends, or they want the 'fun' of a relationship without the commitment." With mathematical precision, she nailed the state of play, at least within the universe of her business school: "The odds are good, but the goods are odd." Poised at the threshold of her 30s, and with another personal goal fulfilled, Susan is ready for marriage, but this doesn't mean that a marriage partner is ready for her. She has headed into a demanding new entrepreneurial venture where she will have to put in long hours and where she is not likely to have convenient opportunities to meet men. "It's starting to sink in. I'm not seeing anyone right now. There's no one in my life. And I think I would have to know someone for two years before I marry, so that means I'll be 31. And that assumes that I will meet someone in the next few months, which doesn't look likely at the moment."

Christina and Susan, the appealing and accomplished young women we've met in these chapters, have succeeded in meeting their personal and career development goals. Now they have reached the stage of life where they are ready for marriage. However, they realize that they face a challenge. It isn't enough to expect Mr. Not Ready to turn into someone who is ready to marry and rear children or Mr. Right to drop into their work lives. They have to think more self-consciously about how to find a marriage-minded and marriageable man. The popular advice tells them to "put yourself out there," but it is hard to follow the advice until you have some sense of where the opportunities lie.

They have few models that can provide answers. They can't follow the path their mothers took from school into early marriage. They are already past the age at which many of their mothers married. Nor do many single women want to follow in the footsteps of a generation of baby boom women, many of whom married in their early 20s and were divorced in their mid-30s, with two children to bring up on an administrative assistant's income. These young women are determined to achieve personal independence, economic self-sufficiency, and career advancement before they set out to find a mate.

This is a wise approach for women who want to marry in the future. The pursuit of education and career is likely to increase their chances of being successful in marriage. Women with at least a baccalaureate degree are more likely to marry and less likely to separate or divorce once they do marry than women with lower levels of educational attainment.[16] What's more, higher education provides women with what they see as divorce insurance. The effects of the divorce revolution of the '70s and '80s have made women more aware of the shakiness of marriage today, and of their economic vulnerability if they divorce. Moreover, higher education gives women a route to economic self sufficiency in the event that they never marry.

And finally, because women today are able to lead independent lives, they are less likely to succumb to pressures to marry the wrong man for the wrong reasons. Indeed, many of the single women I've encountered say that they see too many bright, talented women lowering their standards just for the sake of "being with someone." They'd rather be single than be coupled up with the wrong man. Several told me that they viewed their single status as a sign not of their inability to attract a mate, but of their unwillingness to relax their high standards.

One New York single professional, tired of the rude question "Why aren't you married?" has developed a standard response: "Because I am picky." "And I am," she explains. "I guess I'm like Jane Austen's heroines; all of them (except Emma) have little or no fortune yet turn down the boring or unfortunate-but-responsible match for a love match, which luckily turns out to be a very good match fortunewise as well. I always joke that I'm looking for my Henry Tilney (the hero of *Northanger Abbey* [1818], Austen's early and posthumously published novel), but it wasn't reading about the fictional Henry Tilney that raised my standards; they were always high. Henry just reflects them. He's smart, funny, tall, athletic, almost handsome, reads books, is not filthy rich but makes a good living. He's what I've always looked for and unfortunately have not found."

In trying to make their way in the world of love, young women are now very much on their own. There are no models to follow or guides to direct them. In their school and work lives, women are able to turn to institutional protections or to seek legal remedies if they face unfair or discriminatory practices. But these protections don't carry over into dating. Affirmative action will not turn men into kinder, gentler lovers or more ardent monogamists. Title IX cannot level the playing field in love. And the kind of well-defined and socially supported path that leads women toward success in their work lives is notably missing when they seek to fulfill their ambitions for lasting love.

CHAPTER III

THE NEW SINGLE WOMAN

THE PLIGHT OF TODAY'S ACCOMPLISHED young women arises in the realm of love and marriage, but its origins lie elsewhere. To understand the source of their romantic discontent, it's necessary to begin by looking at their lives, and especially at the patterns of school and work in their early adult lives. Indeed, in unexpected ways, the timetable that leads to precocious success in school and work can change the timetable of their love lives as well.

Today's young educated single woman has become a familiar figure on the social landscape. She's a presence on the streets of nearly every big city. She's the stylish young woman in black, a tote bag slung over her shoulder and a cell phone pressed to her ear, talking and gesturing as she makes her way down Wall Street or K Street or Newbury Street or any other major urban thoroughfare. You can spot her in other places as well: Barnes & Noble, Gold's Gym, Starbucks, Pilates or yoga class. She's attracted to the city because she shares its metabolism. Both run on energy, excitement, novelty, talk, and espresso highs. It's a brilliant alliance: an aspiring Alpha Female hooked up with an Alpha city.

On the other hand, she's something of a mystery. She's doesn't fit any of the old stereotypes of a single woman. She isn't the middle-aged executive secretary, a chaste old maid who is everybody's confidante at work, somebody's favorite aunt at home, and nobody's sweetheart. She isn't the working girl depicted in Helen Gurley Brown's 1962 bestseller, *Sex and the Single Girl*, a high school graduate and "mouseburger" who moves to the city in the hopes of attracting a Big Cheese. She's not the underemployed Girl Friday of the late 1960s, a Seven Sisters' graduate who toils for a few years in publishing before she leaves New York for marriage and an ivied Georgian in Westchester.

Yet though she is easy to spot and hard to place, this young woman is as much a symbol of her times as the Flapper in the 1920s or Rosie the Riveter in the 1940s or the Libber in the 1960s. Like these earlier figures, she has attained cultural prominence and social significance as the model of progressive womanhood. But her distinctive model of progress is based not on social rebellion, like the Flapper, or nontraditional work, like Rosie, or political protest, like the Libber. She embodies a new model of success based on educational and professional achievement.

What the old stereotypes of the single woman had in common was that they defined such women by the absence of marriage. But today's new single woman no longer fits this pattern. What defines her is not her relationship to marriage, but the remarkable path she follows virtually from cradle to career. This path is something new, a life-course pattern that guides young women through almost three decades of life and provides the operating manual for her early adulthood. More than anything else, it is this path that shapes the identity and aspirations of the new single woman and explains her myriad contents and her one manifest discontent.

A NEW MODEL FOR SUCCESS

FOR CENTURIES, OF COURSE, SUCCESS for most young women meant marriage and then motherhood. This was true even for many of the women who came of age in the '60s and early '70s. Back then, the median age of first marriage hovered around age 21 for women. The iconic image for this model of female success was the young bride. In millions of family households, her bridal portrait was displayed on the mantel or the wall as a testament to the defining achievement of her life. Its symbolic significance was clear. It proclaimed to the world: "This is our successful daughter."

Now, the portrait of the successful daughter is more likely to be connected to one or more of her singular accomplishments. In one family, the portrait might say: "This is our successful daughter developing new water systems in Ghana." In another, it might say: "This is our successful daughter during her research fellowship year in St. Petersburg." In yet another, it might proclaim: "This is our successful daughter training for the Olympic biathalon."

Indeed, the iconic image of this new model of female success is the photo negative of the old. The bride is swathed in yards of white. The single wears minimalist black. In the old image, the bride is frozen in time and space. In the new, the single moves in a blur. The bride is clutching a bouquet of cut flowers. The single totes an assortment of wired business tools. The bride is nestled among family and kin. The single connects to a global network.

It is not an exaggeration to say that today's young single woman represents something quite new under the sun. In Western history, only a handful of the most privileged or exceptionally gifted women—abbesses, heiresses, artists, princesses, and courtesans—have been able to establish and lead independent lives as unmarried women. And to achieve this kind of independent adulthood, these women usually had to rely on family fortunes, male sponsors, or the resources attached to departed husbands. Abbesses used dowries to gain positions of influence in the Church; heiresses gained wealth from deceased fathers or spouses; princesses relied on their blood ties to royalty; courtesans cultivated rich male patrons and lovers. Even Elizabeth I, the Virgin Queen, one of the most educated, canny, and powerful unmarried women in history, had to spend much of her reign trying to convince the all-male Privy Council that her dalliances and flirtations were all aimed at making a politically advantageous marriage. And these powerful women were usually well past their early adult years when they achieved independence.

Today's new single woman is neither virgin nor queen, but she is able to achieve something that even powerful women in the past fell short of: an independence that rests largely or completely on her own accomplishments as well as her own resources. Even more remarkable, she achieves this goal at a young age. The new single woman is able to live and work independently, not in her fading 50s, but during her 20s and 30s, at a time of life when she is still in the bloom of youth, beauty, and sexual allure.

THE FEMALE TAKEOVER OF HIGHER EDUCATION

THE STORY OF THE NEW SINGLE woman begins with her remarkable ascendancy into First Sex status in higher education. In a strikingly short period of time, young women have become the majority on undergraduate college campuses. A series of milestone years mark their advance. In 1976, for the first time, the female percentage of June high school graduates who went straight on to college exceeded the percentage of male graduates to do so.[1] In 1981, for the first time, the number of women who received bachelor's degrees exceeded the number of men who earned that degree.[2] In 1984, for the first time, the number of women enrolled in graduate school exceeded the number of men.[3] In 1987, for the first time, the number of women earning master's degrees exceeded the number of men who earned the degree.[4]

Currently, among those who are ages 25 to 39, the number of women who hold at least a bachelor's degree now exceeds the number of men at the same level of educational attainment. Moreover, in some of the traditional "male" fields of study, women have reversed or narrowed the gender gap in baccalaureate degrees. In biology/life sciences, the number of women now exceeds men. In business, women are coming very close to parity with men. And many engineering and computer science departments are offering full-ride scholarships and other inducements to attract bright women to their disciplines.

Today, with the exception of some engineering schools, all-male schools, and most Ivy League schools, female dominance on the undergraduate level has become virtually the norm. A few years ago, *U.S. News & World Report* stated that "the college gender gap has widened at virtually every type of school: large and small, public and private, two-year and four-year . . . from the University of New Mexico (57 percent female) to 2,032-student Catholic-affiliated Edgewood College in Wisconsin (73 percent female) to the mammoth University of California (seven of the eight campuses have female majorities)."[5] At the University of Georgia, a school whose mascot is the bulldog and whose football team is part of a proud collegiate tradition, the entering undergraduate class in 2000 was almost 60 percent female. Betty Bulldog is now Top Dog on campus. Even among the elite schools where men still hold the lead, it is not at all clear how long they will remain in the majority. At Harvard, for example, women now account for about 46 percent of the undergraduate enrollment. Dartmouth, the last of the eight Ivies to go coed in 1972, is 49 percent female, according to the 2001 undergraduate enrollment figures.[6]

Women outperform men academically during their undergraduate years according to one standard measure of achievement. In 1992-93, 61 percent of women who earned bachelor's degrees had GPAs of 3.0 or higher, compared to 49 percent of men.[7] And according to anecdotal evidence, women undergraduates tend to be more focused, better organized, and more disciplined in their academic pursuits than many of their male peers. As a professor at a public university in the Northeast put it, "The men come into class with their backward baseball caps and the 'word processor ate my homework' excuses. Meanwhile, the women are checking their day planners and asking for recommendations for law school."

Women are also more likely to use the world as their classroom. According to a 1998 study, the percentage of women who participated in international study programs was close to twice that of men, 65 percent compared to 35 percent of men.[8] And though the junior year abroad has long been a tradition for coeds, the scope of international studies has expanded far beyond the precincts of Paris, Rome, or London—or even the Western world.

One collegiate T-shirt, carrying the logo "Been There, Done That," lists international study programs in Dar es Saalam, Guanajuato, Olomouc, Pune, and Harare. In a global economy and multicultural society, this kind of experience is a career asset as well as an academic advantage. It builds on women's traditional strength in languages, and it also gives them a credential that is attractive to future employers.

The female takeover of higher education has been propelled by a dramatic expansion of opportunities for girls in secondary schools. The American high school experience has become far more girl-friendly over the past 30 or so years. It is more supportive of girls' academic success, more committed to equity of access in such "boy" subjects as science, math, and sports; and more pro-girl in its school culture. This is not true for all high schools across the country, of course, but it is a significant and pervasive trend in many high schools, especially those that serve middle class or upper class students.

The affluent suburbs, and especially those ringing major metropolitan areas, also provide a start-early academic track for girls, beginning with private preschools—Montessoris, Waldorfs, and country day schools—and continuing up through academically demanding private and public middle schools. (There are 29 Montessoris alone in the Maryland suburbs ringing Washington, D.C., including a bilingual Montessori Academy with programs in Italian, French, and Spanish.)[9] Such schools tend to be in the vanguard of progressive educational trends, especially in their offerings of special gender equity programs designed to boost girls' academic achievement in math, science, and technology. And they provide a feeder system into the elite private secondary schools and into colleges.

In addition, many Gen-X women, as well as the younger girls who are following behind them, are the beneficiaries of what might be called the prepping of the public high school. In the upscale communities and suburbs, today's public schools are looking a lot like private prep schools. Driven by the race for admission to top colleges, by parental ambitions and affluence, by the well-founded association between college graduation and economic success, and by Chamber of Commerce pressures to sell the high quality of local schools to prospective home buyers, high schools have responded by ramping up their academic standards and offerings. They've created special academic programs for the advanced, talented, and gifted, established international study opportunities, boosted school participation in math and music competitions, expanded their athletic facilities, designed programs to encourage participation in nontraditional Olympic sports, and created opportunities for advanced high school students to take courses at nearby colleges.

Nowhere is the prepping of the public high school more evident than in the growing popularity of Advanced Placement courses. The AP program, established and run by the College Board, was created in 1955 to give a select group of mostly male prep school students a head start in college. Back then, these elite students enrolled in a more demanding, collegelike course of study in one or more of their high school subjects and then took an achievement test. If they received a good score, they could then get college credit or placement in a more advanced college course. The popularity of AP grew over the next decades; between 1960 and 1990, the number of students taking AP exams rose from 10,531 students in 1960 to 800,000 in 2001.[10] Among this population, the percentage of female AP test-takers has steadily increased. In 1985, 35 percent were female. In 2001, they made up 45 percent of AP test-takers. In traditional areas of female academic excellence, such as English, foreign languages, history, government, and biology, women now represent the majority of test-takers. Men still have an edge over women in AP tests in math and the sciences, but women are closing the gap. In 2001, for example, females made up 44 percent of AP chemistry test-takers, compared to 31 percent in the mid-1980s.[11]

The popularity of girls' schools in recent years is another indicator of the growing emphasis on an academic fast track for girls. Nationwide, applications and enrollments are increasing, in what the 90-member National Coalition of Girls' Schools describes as a "renaissance" in girls-only education. Nationally, since 1991, the average number of applications to girls' schools has increased 32 percent.[12] In New York, the competition for admission to girls' schools approaches a "frenzy," according to a 1999 *New York Times* story. Applications to Manhattan's private girls' schools have increased 69 percent since 1991; among seven private girls' schools there were ten applications for every kindergarten opening for the fall of 2000.[13] In addition to a rise in enrollments, there has also been a trend toward the establishment of new girls' schools. In just a three-year period, between 1995-98, 14 new schools for girls were founded.[14]

One of the advantages of girls' schools, their promoters say, is that they offer opportunities for girls to excel in traditional "boy" subjects and activities without any competition from boys. The National Coalition of Girls' Schools website offers a checklist to help parents determine whether their daughters should attend a girls' school, including: "Are girls' sports as valued and supported as those for boys? Do girls persist and excel in higher level math and science classes?" "I just didn't want to ruin my daughter's feistiness," one satisfied mother of a kindergartner at Nightingale-Bamford told the *New York Times.* "If she wants to be president of the country, who am I to ruin her chance by having her overshadowed by some boy?"[15]

THE HIGH SCHOOL CAREERS OF THE Gen-X women I interviewed were shaped by these changes. Many had graduated from an elite secondary school. These schools covered a broad spectrum, from private boarding schools to public scholarship schools to magnet schools to Catholic girls' schools to international schools to highly ranked public high schools in affluent suburbs. Included in the mix were graduates from private schools such as Sidwell Friends and the National Cathedral School in Washington, D.C., Northfield Mount Hermon and Milton Academy in Massachusetts, a public magnet school in Raleigh-Durham, North Carolina, Winston Churchill H.S. in Bethesda, Maryland, the International Baccalaureate Program at Winter Park H.S. in Winter Park, Florida, international schools in Hong Kong, and a Catholic girls' school in Peru.

Asked to describe their academic program in high school, most women mentioned a full complement of AP courses and a demanding, sometimes grueling, set of expectations and class work. Some experienced intense competition: one young woman, who began an elite program in a public high school in the ninth grade with 75 classmates, saw almost half drop out before their senior year. For a few, the academic stresses of high school caused them to downshift in their academic performance during their college years. However, for the most part, these young women saw their early academic achievements as an advantage. They got into elite colleges. What's more, they entered college with confidence that they could do well. As one private school graduate told me, "I had classes with the most gifted students, the best teachers, and the hardest exams." After that experience, she didn't have to worry about college courses. In addition, a few women were able to finish college in less than four years, or take time out of college, because their AP preparation helped them pass the achievement tests and thus skip the required 101 courses.

Along with AP academic work, playing team sports was a common denominator for a number of these women. Popular sports included lacrosse, soccer, baseball, field hockey, and basketball. One woman among this group made it into the ranks of elite student athletes as a whitewater sea kayaker. Megan, now 29 and a lawyer on the West Coast, began to kayak at summer camp when she was barely in her teens. She was good at it, thought it was a lot of fun, and soon became part of a group of kayakers who were mostly teenage boys ages 16 to 25. She attended an elite prep school where she had to juggle her training with her school life. She would get up in the morning very early to get out on the water, go to classes, and then, after classes were over, head to either rugby or soccer practice, depending on the season. In addition, she had to squeeze in a training regimen of running and lifting. In her junior year, the hectic pace caught up with her; she got sick and had to give up team sports. However, she continued to work hard at whitewater sea kayaking. Each of two successive summers, she entered the Junior World Championship competition and won it both times. Sports gave her a sense of independence and self-confidence, she says, and an intense "bonding" experience with a group of other elite athletes. It also gave her the opportunity to travel widely, to train in Costa Rica, and to learn Spanish.

Girls' progress in educational attainment would likely have been slower if parents had not invested heavily in their academic preparation and college success. This, too, represents a change. In the past, when it came to preparing their offspring for successful adult lives, many parents adhered to an educational double standard. The boys got a college and sometimes graduate training, and the girls got a wedding. Of course, this generalization overstates the case. In decades past, as today, many parents sent their bright daughters off to college and encouraged them to excel academically. But they often conveyed, in both subtle and not-so-subtle ways, that the ultimate success for daughters was marriage and the ultimate success for sons was a professional career. Perhaps the most significant change in the rearing of girls has to do with the role of fathers' involvement in their daughters' lives. Fathers today play an active part in shaping and promoting their daughters' interests and career ambitions. Hugh Hefner may have been one of the most unlikely fathers to turn the running of his business over to his capable daughter, but he is certainly not alone. Charles Schwab's daughter, Carrie

Schwab Pomeroy, heads up a special initiative for women investors in the financial service company. Muhammad Ali's and Joe Frazier's daughters carry on their fathers' boxing rivalry and legacy. Fathers' employers and job contacts now translate into opportunities for their well-qualified daughters. One woman, whose father was an IBM executive, landed a Tom Watson internship at her father's company. Another father challenged his daughter to take a summer job selling books door-to-door. She discovered that she had an aptitude for marketing, and she went on to become a marketing executive. And like sons in the past, women now choose to take up their fathers' professions. One young woman, estranged from her divorced father, became reconciled with him when she chose to follow in his footsteps and become a lawyer. Another, who admired her father's success as a businessman, got an MBA and then started a new venture with her dad as a partner.

A POST–VAGINA MONOLOGUE GENERATION

SOMETHING ELSE IS NEW ABOUT TODAY'S young single: she's grown up after the sexual revolution, and sex has been a part of her conscious awareness ever since girlhood. From her earliest years, she's been enlightened about sex. Conscientious parents and teachers have stuffed her head with advice, admonition, and formal instruction in improper touching, sexuality, contraception, condoms, STDs, sexual molestation, the risks of unprotected sex, and date rape with the goal, in the words of one sex education book, to be "healthy, safe, and in charge." As historian Joan Jacobs Brumberg notes, "Middle class girls of ten and eleven are socialized into a world where sexuality is regarded as absolutely normal but also rather perilous."[16] She's also had an informal schooling in sex from the media, women's fashion magazines, and her peers. By the time she reaches high school, she's learned to be frank and open about sexual matters in coed company, to talk about her sexual needs in a matter-of-fact way that would have made earlier generations of teenage girls blush. She doesn't "get" baby boom women's exhilaration over discussing private parts in public. She belongs to the post–Vagina Monologue generation.

Another distinguishing feature for this new single woman: sex is likely to be pleasurable, exciting, and a way to express love, but it is not as closely connected to marriage as it was for earlier generations of young women. For older women, premarital sex was truly premarital: the timing of first sexual intercourse was closely connected to the timing of first marriage. Ninety percent of women born between 1933-42 were either virgins when they married or had first intercourse with the man they wed. Among women born in the 1960s, only 10 percent were married when they first had sex.[17] Today, first sex and first marriage are often separated by nearly a decade, or more. For young women today, the average age of first sexual intercourse is 17 and the median age of first marriage is 25. Since college-educated professional women are likely to marry at later ages, the gap between the two milestone events can be even greater.

Most likely, today's young single had sex for the first time in her late teens. By the time she leaves college, she's had one or more serious relationships that included sex. She expects to have sex as part of normal dating relationships, and because she is spending more years as a dating single before marriage, she is likely to have more sexual partners than, say, a woman who marries in her early 20s. This isn't to say that she's having frequent one-night stands or anonymous sex, but she does have sex with men she feels affection for, as well as with some she doesn't.

Researchers at the University of Chicago, who have conducted the most reliable sex survey of American adults currently available, provide a snapshot portrait of women's sexual partners over a one-year period. Among never-married women ages 18 to 29, 12.9 percent had no sexual partner in the past 12 months; 56.6 percent had one sexual partner; 24.2 percent had 2 to 4 partners; and only 6.2 percent had five or more partners. Among those ages 30 to 44, 37.3 percent had no sexual partner in the past year; 42.4 percent had one partner; 17.8 percent had 2 to 4; and only 2.5 percent had 5 or more partners. Formerly married women show slightly higher percentages of multiple partners in the past year, but otherwise the pattern is similar to never-married women in the same age group. For those ages 18 to 29, 2.0 percent had no partners; 58.8 percent report one partner; 33.3 percent 2 to 4 partners; 5.9 percent, five or more. Those ages 30 to 44, and formerly married: 18.9 percent; 58.3 percent; 21.7 percent; 1.1 percent.[18]

The more educated the individual, the more partners they have over a lifetime. This isn't because educated people have "a sex drive in overdrive," according to the authors of *Sex in America*, a popular treatment of the University of Chicago survey.[19] It has to do with the timing of entry into first marriage. People with more education are also more likely to put off marriage until they finish their schooling and get traction in their career. Today, of course, when the median age of first marriage may be closer to 27 or 28 than to 25 for college-educated women, these women are likely to have more sex partners because they spend a larger proportion of their early adult life as never-married or divorced singles.

Along with the social climate of sexual freedom has come a new social openness toward young single women's sexual behavior. In times past, a socially respectable young never-married woman was expected to be chaste, or to maintain the appearance and reputation of chastity. If she did otherwise, she risked social ostracism, scandal, and perhaps reduced chances for an advantageous marriage. It was commonly thought that a sexually active single woman posed a threat to the community, to the institution of marriage, and to married women. Today, however, the commonly held view is that single women's sexuality, properly and responsibly managed, poses no larger threat or disruption to the social order. Today's single woman can be as open and frank as she chooses about her sexual relationships without risk of social disgrace. Whatever she chooses to do in her sex life, she runs little chance of scandal (unless she chooses to have sex with a famous married politician, and even then, she may get an interview with Barbara Walters and her own brand-name line of jeans or hand-bags). She is also able to have a child on her own without social disapproval if she is able to provide economically for the child.

But this sketch only begins to capture what is most striking about such new single women. One common thread runs throughout their experience: they've been on a strenuous path to achievement since girlhood. Today's single women are like specimen orchids. They've been bred to win prizes.

A REVOLUTION IN GIRL-REARING

THE NEW SINGLE WOMAN DID not appear by accident. She's emerged at this moment in history as the result of a self-conscious and highly successful social project whose chief purpose is to prepare young women for adult lives of economic self-sufficiency, social independence, and sexual liberation. Call it the Girl Project.

The Girl Project began just 30 years ago. At the time, hardly anyone could have foretold how quickly it would catch on or how widely it would spread. Yet in that brief period of time, it has transformed patterns of girl-rearing and altered the early adult lives of an ever growing number of women. So far, its widest and deepest impact has been on women who were born after the mid-1960s, entered their teens after the 1970s, and earned their bachelor's degrees after 1990. Today, the ranks of such women make up a critical mass among college-educated females under the age of 35.

The Girl Project set forth a goal that is new in the tradition of girl-rearing. Rather than prepare girls for future adult lives as wives and mothers, the Girl Project's aim has been to prepare them for adult lives without dependence on marriage. It's not that the Girl Project challenges marriage per se, or the desire for marriage. Rather, it creates an alternate path to acquiring many of the assets and benefits that were once bundled into a single institution called marriage. This path relies on higher education and early career development. If young women follow this alternate path, they can get satisfying work, a good income, sex, a nest, and a nest egg of their own—and all without marriage.

This new path to independence is strikingly different from the old path that led to marriage. For one thing, it takes longer to complete. It starts earlier in a girl's life, perhaps as early as age two or three and lasts longer, at least through the mid-20s, and, depending on a woman's chosen career or profession, possibly into the early 30s. For another, on the old path, there was no separate stage in early adult life devoted to singlehood. The period of time between the end of school and entry into first marriage was brief, transitional, and premarital. For most women, the years of single life were a fleeting interregnum between graduation day and wedding day, a time to gather a beau and a trousseau, to court and to marry. The new path creates an entire life stage, a period of a decade or so that is devoted to living on one's own as an unmarried, though not necessarily unpartnered, single. It combines some of the communal features of college life with the new responsibilities of earning a living, paying off college loans, and gaining some measure of financial and residential stability.

Further, the new path sets forth a more demanding set of hurdles and a more strenuous pace. The marriage path trained girls in the domestic arts and educated them in the disciplines and occupations that would mesh with future family lives. These were not especially hard to master. Most girls could learn to cook, grocery shop, and care for children. Even some traditional female professions that took women beyond a high school education—such as nursing or secretarial work—did not require a four-year college degree. The new educational path, on the other hand, stresses precocious performance and achievement, the acquisition of time management and goal-setting skills, early exposure to the world of paid professional work, an academically challenging school career, admission to a good college, a baccalaureate degree, and perhaps a graduate or professional degree as well, and then the successful launching of a professional career.

Finally, the new path cultivates a set of aptitudes and habits of mind that prepare girls for the competitive world of higher education and career. This, too, is a new development. In times past, girls were schooled in the virtues and traits that would attract a suitable mate and prepare them for marriage and motherhood. Such traits included helpfulness, charm, niceness, thrift, patience, personal sacrifice, and forbearance. Today, however, girls are raised to speak up for themselves, to compete and strive for individual excellence, and to take initiative and responsibility for their future economic lives.

THE GIRL PROJECT HAD TWO PRINCIPAL sources of inspiration. One was the feminist vision of an independent life for women rooted in paid professional work. Sixties feminism had started out as a movement to break barriers to adult women's progress in education and the paid workforce, but by the 1970s, its leaders saw similar obstacles in the lives of girls. Girls faced barriers to their full participation in sports; they had to deal with anti-girl biases in mathematics and science; their talents and ambitions were cramped by the narrow set of career options that were deemed suitable for girls. Consequently, feminists began to carry the struggle for gender equity into the realm of girl-rearing. From the 1970s on, feminist energies and initiatives turned to the task of breaking the barriers to girls' educational progress and to readying girls for successful lives in the paid professional work place.

The second major inspiration for the Girl Project was the divorce revolution. During the 1970s, as state after state adopted no-fault divorce laws, the divorce rate began to climb steeply until it reached a historic high in the early 1980s before dropping slightly to current levels. (According to the latest Census Bureau projections, the risk of divorce remains extremely high—50 percent of first marriages are projected to end in divorce.[20]) As scholars now agree, this revolution had a profound impact on children, and on many divorcing adults. But its legacy extended far beyond divorcing partners and even beyond the children of divorced parents. Divorce was to Gen-X what Vietnam was to the baby boom. It shaped the outlook of an entire generation.

It also had an impact on the thinking about how to prepare girls for successful adult lives. More than just a social trend, divorce was also a social teacher. As such, it conveyed one indelible lesson: namely, that marriage is unreliable as an economic partnership and precarious as a life vocation for women. Far from being a safe bet, it taught, marriage is a gamble. Moreover, the gamble was riskiest, and the losses heaviest, for traditional wives who stayed out of the paid work force for long stretches of time and invested all their talents, energies, and identities in marriage and children. When such family-primary women got divorced, as a growing number did during the 1970s and 1980s, their economic fortunes plummeted, their social identity as a wife vanished, their sense of self-worth dropped, at least for a time.

The social lessons of divorce made a strong impression on parents of young daughters, as well as on teachers, girls' advocates, and youth leaders who were directly involved in preparing the next generation of girls for successful adult lives. In a world where five out of ten marriages were projected to end in divorce, it no longer seemed to make sense to prepare girls for lives as wives, even if they were college-educated wives with teaching, social work, or nursing degrees to fall back on. Instead of relying on marriage for economic security and social identity, it seemed more practical and realistic to prepare girls for lives of economic self-sufficiency and social independence.

In response, a project to reform the practices of rearing girls began to take shape. Its purpose was to build a better girl, or to be more precise, to build a girl who was armored against the instability of marriage, or the chances that she might never marry. Through education, girls could gain the credentials and competencies that were portable and inalienable. The advantages of this approach seemed obvious. As some warned, your prince might never come, or he might come with a bad credit rating and a wandering eye.[21] But no one could take away what was in your head or on your transcript and resumé.

Feminists lit the spark for this project, but parents, teachers, girls' organizations, and other adults directly involved in rearing girls fanned the flames. As a result, the Girl Project spread from a narrow feminist initiative into a broad-based overhaul of girl-rearing practices. In the span of three decades, the Girl Project shaped a new social consensus about what girls look like, what they stand for, and what they can achieve in their lives. It helped to write what amounts to a new social curriculum for girl-rearing and to institutionalize this curriculum for future generations of girls. And it recruited social support and sympathy for the new path to independence.

IF THERE IS A DATE THAT MARKS THE official beginning of the Girl Project, it is 1972. That year, President Richard Nixon, the father of two daughters, signed Title IX of the Omnibus Education Amendments into law. Title IX was not originally aimed at preventing discrimination against girls, but at preventing discrimination against adult women. However, once Title IX passed, women's organizations soon recognized that the measure could be applied to discrimination against girls. The parallel between obstacles to success for women and obstacles to success for girls seemed obvious. Just as women were held back by legal and institutional inequities in the workplace, girls experienced the same kind of difficulties in their version of the "workplace"—the public school.

Thus, the Girl Project initially followed a classic civil rights model. It sought to establish equal rights for girls through the law. Feminists led the fight to break the barriers to girls' equal access and participation in school and community sports. The first celebrated application of Title IX to girls came in 1973, when the National Organization for Women won its suit to admit girls to Little League baseball. This famous case not only gave girls the right to play ball. It broke a traditional bastion of boy privilege and established a precedent for the future challenges to discrimination against girls in school and sports.

As a result of the successful legal challenges under Title IX, feminists helped bring about a revolution in girls' sports participation. In the year before the passage of the law, fewer than 300,000 girls were involved in interscholastic sports; by the year 2000, the number exceeded 2.6 million.[22] By 1994, an estimated 8 million girls under 17 played basketball, and nearly as many played soccer.[23] Title IX legal action also brought more funding for girls' sports programs, gym time, coaches, and uniforms. Title IX gave athletically gifted teenage girls new outlets, recognition, and rewards for their talent. Those who excelled in sports got chances for achievement awards and college athletic scholarships. Before Title IX, the money available for women's college athletic scholarships was negligible; today, it exceeds $180 million.[24] Along with these tangible material rewards, Title IX brought school recognition and praise for girl athletes. Girls whose physical talents might have been overlooked, or who might have been teased for being too big or too tall, could now be cheered and high-fived for their strength and size, for their bench presses or batting averages or blocked shots.

But Title IX's impact was not limited to the athletic elite. Even more modestly gifted girls gained attention and mentoring support from coaches, teachers, and other adults who were involved in athletic events and activities. Indeed, Title IX made team sports a standard, if not obligatory part, of the girlhood experience. Symbolically, too, Title IX made a difference. Where girls were situated on a playing field corresponded to where they were situated on the social map. As spectators, they were on the margins; as players, they were at the center of the social map, even if they warmed the bench. In their role as spectators, they were the audience; in their role as players, they had an audience. Moreover, Title IX opened up to girls the repertoire of character traits and values that had once been identified with boys' sports. Girls now had an opportunity to develop physical strength, competitive drive, and team leadership.

However, if the Girl Project had been limited to feminist legal initiatives alone, it might not have won a popular audience. It gained broad grassroots support because it captured the imaginations and sympathies of parents, including a large fan base of fathers. Indeed, through Title IX, the Girl Project shrewdly exploited two of the most powerful and unifying popular sentiments in American life—the love of sports and the love of the underdog competitor.

Much of the grassroots enthusiasm for girls sports came from the suburbs. The affluent suburbs provided an ideal environment for nurturing girls' sports. There was space and money for soccer fields, ice rinks, horse farms, tennis courts, golf courses, Olympic-size pools, fitness centers, and fully equipped gyms. There was also a critical mass of professional parents who could spend money on sports equipment, ice time, and summer training camps. And though these parents had demanding work schedules, they often had more flexibility than parents who punched a clock. They could make themselves available as chauffeurs, coaches, fund raisers, and organizers in "staffing and supporting" their daughters' sports activities.

More than any other sport, soccer became the emblematic girls' game. Its phenomenal growth came during the 1980s and 1990s, as Gen-X girls were coming of age. In 1976–77, only 11,534 high school girls were registered to play soccer; in 1999, when Mia Hamm and her teammates won the Women's World Cup Soccer Championship, that number had risen to 257,586. Add the population of younger soccer-playing girls and this figure soars into the millions. Of the 18 million registered soccer players in the United States, 7.5 million, or 40 percent, were girls and women.[25]

One of the great advantages of soccer was that girls didn't have to fight to earn the right to play in a sport that came with an established boyhood tradition and mythology, like Little League baseball or Pop Warner football. When soccer arrived in the American suburbs, it arrived as a coed sport, and girls soon excelled at it, swiftly climbed into the professional ranks, and then into a new pantheon of soccer superstars. Though there are many superb male soccer players in the United States, there has not yet been a male soccer star who has so captured the popular imagination as Mia Hamm.

Another reason for soccer's success was timing. The sport appeared on the community playing field just as baby boomers were moving to the suburbs and becoming parents. College-educated suburban baby boom parents were especially receptive to progressive ideas about girl-rearing and admiring of girls who challenged gender stereotypes. Among progressive parents, a feisty athletic daughter was a source of pride, whereas a traditionally feminine daughter was a mild social embarrassment. Moreover, for pre-Title IX mothers, who remembered the days of boring girls' gym classes, girls' one-piece gym suits, all-girl booster clubs, and no-girl teams, their daughters' success on the soccer field was yet another sign of women's progress in breaking barriers. In an article celebrating the Women's World Cup Soccer Championship, *Time* magazine columnist Margaret Carlson reflected on the differences between her own girlhood sports experience and that of her post-Title IX daughter. Although Carlson was a tomboy whose dad spent hours playing catch with her, "he never expected that there would be organized softball for girls." However, today, her father sits in the stands and cheers as his granddaughter, suited in the bright gold mesh-and-lycra soccer uniform of the Stoddert Stompers, "went splat into the ground trying to block a goal." "So much of what is wonderful about being a woman in 1999," Carlson enthused, "is embodied in the U.S. women's soccer team."[26]

If girls' soccer awakened mothers' inner goalie, it had an even more profound impact on fathers. In the past, fathers often felt awkward and disconnected from their daughters' girlhood activities and interests, especially as their daughters reached adolescence and turned to traditionally feminine pursuits. But fathers who followed sports and had played sports could identify with daughters who were aspiring jocks. After all, it was easier for fathers to talk to daughters about their blocking skills or hook shots than it was to talk parties, proms, or periods. John Hendricks, Discovery Channel founder and a major investor in the Washington Freedom, one of the new professional women's soccer teams, has an easy explanation for men's strong support for women's professional sports: "Most of us are soccer dads."[27]

There was an unexpected social bonus for fathers in this development as well. In the late 20th-century culture, the father-son relationship was fraught with conflict and tension. Memoirs and biographies poured out tales of post-war fathers whose stern control had drained the life and spirit from their sons. But the new father-daughter relationship won high approval ratings as a culturally progressive role for men. Further, with the decline in the size of families with children, many fathers had daughters only. Fathers could channel their traditional masculine impulses and ambitions into the school and sports careers of their female offspring. It was the ideal combination of Alpha Male nature and Beta Male nurture. (The father-daughter theme appears frequently in advertising for companies such as State Farm Insurance, T. Rowe Price, and Merrill Lynch.)

Soccer appealed to girls as much as to their parents. A beginner did not need exceptionally high skills to play. So almost any girl could take it up, and at an early age. And getting a head start in sports could boost girls' involvement and success in team sports in school later on. What's more, soccer fit girls' hectic after-school schedules: two 45-minute periods (40 for the under-six crowd), post-game treats, and then on to violin lessons. And it was fun, a key motivation for girls to get involved. (According to a number of studies, young girls are attracted to playing sports because it is fun and a social activity, while boys are more oriented to competition and winning.[28])

The scope of the Girl Project included far more than sports, of course. In fact, its chief emphasis was on academic achievement and career readiness. But girls' sports served as a powerful engine to drive the ethos of early achievement and career readiness. And claims of the advantages to girls' sports participation went beyond the fun of playing a game.

Sports helped girls get ahead in school and in life, some studies suggested. A 1997 landmark report issued by the President's Council on Physical Fitness summarized much of the research evidence on the positive impact of sports on the academic achievement and self-image of girls. Girls who played sports achieved at higher academic levels, were more likely to stay in school and go on to college, and avoid the perils that threatened to limit school achievement, such as early sexual involvement or pregnancy, smoking, or taking drugs. In addition, according to this study, sports participation boosted girls' energy, optimism, and self-esteem. Not all the evidence was positive: girl athletes were vulnerable to injuries, burn-out, over-training, addictive exercise, distorted body image, and eating disorders, especially in sports like figure skating, gymnastics, and swimming, where thinness was pushed and prized. But the benefits for most girls far outweighed the risks.[29]

Some researchers linked girls' sports participation to future career success. According to their accounts, sports would not only give girls physical skills; it would also train them in workplace skills such as time management, goal-setting, teamwork, and an orientation to competition and winning. These skills helped women get ahead in professions dominated by men and compete in a work world still largely shaped by male codes of aggression and combat. *See Jane Win*, a study of the girlhood paths followed by older successful women, suggests that participation in sports was a career asset for such women because it taught them how men behaved in competition and team play. According to one woman profiled in the book, a physician who had competed as an elite rower in college, the experience of being one of the guys helped her succeed in a still heavily male-dominated profession: "I was one of two women training with a group of men. Success in this group set the stage to train and compete with male surgeons without carrying any major chips on my shoulder."[30]

The Girl Project also saw sports as a principal means to inculcate a set of more muscular character traits that would foster success in future careers. These traits included physical courage and strength, initiative, assertiveness, competitive spirit, and self-discipline. Such character traits were not entirely alien to girls, of course, but in the past they had been far more identified with, and self-consciously cultivated among, boys. Sports gave girls a chance to break out of the straitjacket of passive, people-pleasing behavior associated with traditional girlhood. Athletic girls could overcome the pressure to be nice and compliant: they could be strong rather than weak, brave rather than fearful, assertive rather than deferential, bold rather than timid, feisty rather than demure.

Nonetheless, these locker-room traits were not simply borrowed wholesale from the boys. The Girl Project successfully combined these new attributes with much of the moral purity and social uplift of the girlhood tradition. Indeed, in this new synthesis, girls' sports stands out as the exemplary counterpoint to boys' sports. According to the popular portrait of the two genders, the differences couldn't be greater. Girls who play sports do better academically; boys who play sports do worse. Girls use sports as a way to avoid sex; boys use sports as a way to get sex. Girls see team sports as a way to pursue more altruistic goals, like winning the fight against breast cancer. Boys see team sports as a way to individual fame, fortune, glory, and endorsement contracts. Girls learn cooperation and teamwork through sports; boys learn violence and misogyny. Similarly, in this gendered mythos, women's professional sports is like a spritz of Lysol on the stink of professional men's sports, with its violence, misogyny, and corruption. As Saskia Webber, the reserve goalie on the U.S. Women's Soccer team puts it, "You're not going to pick up the paper tomorrow and see one of us in it for money-laundering or cocaine use or soliciting. . . . All of us want to be role models, want to be ambassadors."[31]

STRONG IS BEAUTIFUL

THE GIRL PROJECT ALSO INSPIRED a new literature on girl-rearing, and the titles of the books alone tell much of their story. Nearly every one includes one of the four S-words: success, strength, self-esteem, and sports. Representative examples include: *How to Mother a Successful Daughter: A Practical Guide to Empowering Girls from Birth to Eighteen; How to Father a Successful Daughter; Cherishing Our Daughters: How Parents Can Raise Girls to Become Confident Women; Growing a Girl: Seven Strategies for Raising a Strong, Spirited Daughter; Raising Strong Daughters; Sports Her Way: Motivating Girls to Start and Stay with Sports; Girls Seen and Heard: 52 Life Lessons for Our Daughters; Games Girls Play: Understanding and Guiding Young Female Athletes; No More Frogs to Kiss: 99 Ways to Give Economic Power to Girls; Raising Our Athletic Daughters: How Sports Can Build Self-Esteem and Save Girls' Lives; Things Will Be Different for My Daughter: A Practical Guide to Building Her Self-Esteem; Dads and Their Daughters: Father-to-Father Strategies; Any Girl Can Rule the World.*

No collection of girl-rearing books has offered a more authoritative statement of the new girl-rearing principles than the *Girl Scout Handbook*. As it has been written and amended over almost a century, the *Girl Scout Handbook* is the constitution of girlhood; it codifies each generation's ideas about how girls should be prepared for successful adult lives, and it provides one of the most valuable resources for understanding the changing nature and goals of progressive girl-rearing in mainstream America.

Not long ago, I found a 1955 edition of the *Girl Scout Handbook* in my local Salvation Army store. This green-and-black cloth volume ($1.00 a copy) lists proficiency badges under the four main subject areas: adventuring in the arts, citizens here and abroad, fun in the out-of-doors, and you and your home. In 1955, proficiency badges for "You and Your Home" included Homemaker, Cook, Housekeeper, Seamstress, Hospitality, Handywoman.

In the 1955 edition, girls' sports activities were largely limited to individual recreational pursuits: cyclist, swimmer, boating, skating, horsewoman, skiing, tennis, badminton, ping pong, golf, archery, bowling, shuffleboard, paddle tennis, water skiing. Canoeing involved more than one girl, of course, but here the *Girl Scout Handbook* seemed to emphasize the fine arts as much as the physical arts: "learn several songs, the rhythm of which is suited to paddling."

In this long ago world, girls' sports participation focused heavily on reading about, explaining, and organizing sporting activities rather than actually playing sports. Girls had to tackle such tasks as comparing method of play, rules, and formations used in boys' games (baseball, basketball, football, ice hockey) with girls sports; serving as a member of school athletic or games committees; or planning three nutritious lunches suitable for an all-day bicycle trip.

Nearly half a century later, the *Girl Scout Handbook* looks different from the green, cloth-bound, textbooklike edition from the mid-20th century. In fact, today, the *Girl Scout Handbook* is not one handbook, but five separate books, each corresponding to the age-grouped level of scouting. And with the proliferation of books, the number of badges and proficiency areas has changed and also grown. Compared to the 1955 edition, for example, sports are now more physically challenging and team-oriented. The emphasis is on what the leaders call "high adventure sports," and the goal is to teach girls to "gain strength and courage." For the youngest scouts ages 5 to 8, there is a sports readiness program. In the *Junior Girl Scout Badgebook*, aimed at girls ages 8 to 11, sports badges for individual sports include extreme sports, such as hiking, kayaking, rock climbing, and windsurfing, and field sports, including softball, soccer, and lacrosse.

There is also a strong emphasis on researching and exploring nontraditional careers, including 23 in the field of sports alone, and acquiring career-related skills. Junior scouts can also earn badges in Business, Careers, Money Sense, Science Sleuth, and Math Whiz, as well as the more traditional badges in Knot Tying, Child Care, Model Citizen, and Community. The *Cadette Girls Scout Book*, for girls ages 12 to 14, prominently features Life Success Skills, including managing your time, speaking up for yourself, earning and managing money, and preparing for a satisfying career. "Girl Scouting is much more than cookies and camping," the 2001 annual report notes, "today, it teaches girls skills in sports, science and technology, and money management."[32]

Girl Scouting does more than develop a bundle of competencies, however. It tries to build character and to instill values. In this area of girl development, there is continuity in the core values. Since its beginnings nearly a century ago, Girl Scouting has promoted citizenship, voluntarism, and international understanding, along with honesty, fairness, helpfulness, and respect for others. Nonetheless, it is noteworthy that one trait is far more prominent and frequently mentioned today than at any earlier time: it is strength. The Girl Scout Law now includes a pledge to "do my best to be courageous and strong. And the slogan "Helping Girls Grow Strong" has become "a Girl Scout mantra."

THE GIRL PROJECT NOT ONLY FOSTERED strength as a character trait. It also sculpted a new physical image for the American girl that was physically stronger, more active, and more muscular. This image has been brilliantly captured in a photographic exhibit, *Game Face: What Does a Female Athlete Look Like?* The exhibit, which opened at the Smithsonian Institution in Washington, D.C., before its national tour, was the brainchild of *San Francisco Chronicle* sports reporter Jane Gottesman. In the mid-1990s, Gottesman began to keep count of the number of photos of women that ran in her paper's sports section. She discovered that days would go by without a single photo of a woman; when a photo of a female athlete did appear, it was often juxtaposed to the ads for "escort services" that appeared in the pages of the sports section. She also counted the number of *Sports Illustrated* covers that featured women athletes between 1993–4. Other than the annual swimsuit issue, she discovered that women were featured on the cover only when they were being stabbed (Monica Seles), clubbed (Nancy Kerrigan), or bullied (Mary Pierce and her father). Determined to counter these images, she spent several years searching, digging, and culling photographs of girls and women playing sports. The *Game Face* exhibit, and a companion book coauthored with Geoffrey Biddle, is the result of her investigation.[33]

I visited the exhibit shortly after it opened. Some of the photographs featured famous sports figures—Brandi Chastain, jersey off, muscled arms raised in the famous "YES" victory photo at the World Cup soccer match; Gold Medalist sprinter Gwen Torrence, intense, coiled, and still as a statue, as she waits for the starting gun; Chris Evert and Martina Navratilova, biceps bulging, in an arm-wrestling contest. But the show includes many images of girls. The girls in the photographs are bodies in motion: spinning, flying, crouching, running, swimming, diving, jumping; their faces are as mobile as their bodies. They reflect the full range of sports' emotions: effort, concentration, determination, exhaustion, exhilaration—everything but a seductive pout. And though they come in many shapes and sizes, they are strong. One of the most stunning images, and the frontispiece of the exhibit's companion book, shows a short, square girl, in an Adidas jumpsuit, lifting a giant log over her head. Her gaze is direct, her face unsmiling. She's not the princess in a tower: she is the tower.

However, the new physical image of girls is neither traditionally feminine nor androgynously feminist. Instead, it borrows elements from both and comes up with a synthesis of feminine strength. A Nike ad brilliantly captures its essence. It shows a preteen girl, maybe ten or eleven, in her hockey uniform, a devil emblazoned on the jersey. She's pulled her helmet back from her face. Her face is fixed in rapt attention on something that is going on in the game, off camera. Perhaps it's a referee's call or a score by the opposing team or an injury on the ice. It's not clear whether she's just come out of the game or is about to go in, but either way, she's focused and charged up.

The intensity of her expression dominates the full-page ad. But in the upper right-hand corner, in very small typeface, you see the Nike swoosh and three words: "I like pink." The "I like pink" hockey girl exemplifies the synthesis of old and new girl characteristics into what might be called feminist femininity. She isn't trying to imitate the boys or beat the boys. She's playing her own game at the highest level. And she's all girl. In fact, she expresses her femininity in the most traditional way: in her aesthetic appreciation for the classic natal color assigned to girls. Another sports book, aimed at eight- and nine-year-old girls, gives its readers advice on how to affirm this combination of strength and femininity: "If they call you a tomboy, tell them, 'Nope. I'm a strong girl who likes to play sports.'"[31]

THE CULTURAL ASCENDANCY OF GIRLS

THE GIRL PROJECT HAS BEEN A REMARKABLE, if largely unacknowledged, success, and it continues to gain momentum and support to this day. Its accomplishments are impressive. It has boosted girls' presence and achievement in sports. It has propelled women into higher education so rapidly that they have become the first sex in higher education. It has provided stepping stones to careers in fields that once were off-limits to women. It has recruited widespread social support and sympathy for its goal of preparing girls for independent adult lives. It has changed the consensus on what are socially desirable attributes and virtues of young womanhood. It has revolutionized the goals of young women's early adult life course and transformed the path women follow into early adulthood.

Almost everywhere you look today, from Lisa Simpson to 16-year-old Olympic Gold medalist Sarah Hughes, there is evidence of the cultural ascendancy of girls. And evidence of girls' remarkable achievements and feats are hardly limited to cartoons or celebrities. Last Valentine's Day, my hometown newspaper ran a profile of an outstanding teenage girl. The hook for the holiday-themed profile was the teenager's name: Valentina Valentini. According to the story, however, this bright 18-year-old, whose name conjures images of double-dip helpings of love, disdains the holiday devoted to romance as "too false and sentimental." Instead, she dedicates herself to work—and working out. She starts many of her days on the Connecticut River at 5:00 A.M. so that she can row with a crew team. (Her high school doesn't have a crew team so she got a job with the local Women's Rowing Club. She also landed a spot as the honorary guest coxswain for the University of Massachusetts men's crew team.) She spends her mornings at high school, taking AP classes in French, math, and history. By noon, she finishes and heads over to Amherst College where she takes a political science class. (Last semester she studied Italian at the University of Massachusetts.) She sings in the school chorale, performs in dance programs (12 years of ballet), acts in the high school musical, and travels to Japan as part of the Amherst Community Theater troupe. She is also a "pop-alternative" singer with a professional manager and a recording date coming up soon. If that sounds like a full plate, it's only a second or third course. She also works 20 hours at a local coffee house and works out at a fitness center three times a week. And she's just back from the National Youth Leadership Forum on Law, one of 350 students selected to participate in a weeklong round of visits to law firms, courthouses, and law schools. Next, she'll spend a week in Washington as a member of the National Young Leaders Conference. "I'm very well-organized," she says. "I have an assignment book and a day planner."[35]

THE CHANGING TIMETABLE FOR LOVE

LIKE YOUNG VALENTINA, THE GIRL Project's single-minded focus has been on achievement. It has established and supported a fast-paced timetable to school and work success. This timetable comes with social and educational support. It has a clear set of operating instructions and rules. It aims at fairness, gender equity, and a level playing field.

The advantages of such a support system are evident. In the past, when there were fewer institutional or social supports for girls' talents and nontraditional ambitions, it was much harder. Relatively few could achieve as much at such an early stage in life, and even those exceptional young women had to overcome daunting obstacles along the way. Today, strong social, legal, and institutional protections and supports have reduced or cleared away the obstacles to individual achievement. Thanks to the Girl Project, an ever growing number of young women have been able to realize their talents and full potential.

At the same time that the Girl Project has created a new timetable for work, it has also changed the timetable for love. For the cum laude graduates of the Girl Project, the season of true love often comes later than it once did for college-educated women. When these women begin to turn their thoughts and attentions to the search for a life mate, they are not 18-year-old college coeds. They are accomplished, sophisticated, working singles in their 20s and 30s. They have a surer sense of who they are and what they want in a future life mate. But they aren't spending their time in an age-segregated college campus world where it is easy to meet peer men. They're out in a more diverse working adult world.

Thus, when their thoughts and priorities focus on finding someone they would want to spend their life with, they don't find the kind of supportive social system for their love lives that they've enjoyed in their school and early work lives. The process of finding a life partner is often chaotic, unintelligible, and full of unexpected twists. There are no common standards or codes of behavior. There are few models or mentors. There is no operating manual that provides instruction or guidance. There is no institutional infrastructure to make it easier to realize their goals.

This is because the world of love itself is currently undergoing profound change. At the very time that the new single woman is entering her prime years for seeking and finding a life mate, the long-established system of romantic courtship and marriage that once served college educated women like her is fading, and a new system is rising in its place.

CHAPTER IV

THE RISE OF A
RELATIONSHIPS SYSTEM

IN WESTERN SOCIETIES, A SYSTEM of romantic courtship and marriage has governed mate selection for centuries. This type of mating system is relatively rare in human societies. Most of the societies in the world today, as well as in the past, have some form of arranged marriage. Third parties, usually parents or kin groups, play a major role in choosing a mate for offspring, and in negotiating the conditions for the marriage. And typically, the wealthier the family, the more influence parents and kin have over mate selection.

What makes the Western system so unusual is that it gives young men and women the responsibility and freedom to choose their own marriage partner based on considerations of mutual affection and emotional compatibility, rather than on family or power interests. For this reason, the system that has dominated mating in the West places an extremely high premium on the courtship process by which the young freely choose a marriage mate. Although other mating systems include various forms of wooing and lovemaking, this system has sought to promote and regularize romantic courtship. It has established norms, practices, and occasions that help men and women meet, get to know each other, learn about each other's character, habits, and interests. It has carved out leisure time for the young to socialize. It has encouraged a lengthy period of social interaction between men and women as a prelude to the choice of marriage partner. It has supported the development of distinctive social occasions and meeting places for the young. Indeed, the balls, assemblies, card parties, county assizes, as well as the social seasons at Bath and London, so familiar to readers of Jane Austen, were self-conscious social innovations in 18th-century England, explicitly designed to promote courtship among the English upper class young.[1] And as Austen biographer Claire Tomalin notes, the novelist herself relished such balls and parties, while slyly mocking their purpose in her novels: "To be fond of dancing," Austen writes in *Pride and Prejudice*, "was a certain step toward falling in love."[2] Cultivation of romantic courtship continued from the 18th century until the last third of the 20th century. In both English and American societies, there were family, social, and institutional supports for a system of youthful courtship, though this system was increasingly mediated by an adolescent peer culture in the 20th century.

Although this system of romantic courtship and marriage has been remarkably durable, it has lost much of its influence over sexual and romantic relationships in recent decades. Changes in sexual mores and behavior, a persistently high rate of divorce, historic increases in unwed childbearing, the resort to new reproductive and matchmaking technologies, the rise of cohabitation as an opposite-sex union, and the decline of college-based courtship are all signs of the weakening of this long-established system.

To be sure, some of its features, such as the youthful aspiration to lifelong marriage and the cultural ideal of affectionate friendship within marriage, remain remarkably strong and enduring. Indeed, among young adults today, this cultural ideal has risen to an even higher level. Men and women alike say they want to marry a "soul mate," someone who fulfills their needs and desires at a sexual, emotional, and spiritual level.[3] Even so, there is little doubt that we are going through a time of social upheaval in the established system. A new and different system has emerged and taken its place alongside the long-established one.

THE TWO MATING SYSTEMS

IN BROAD OUTLINE, THE KEY FEATURES of the two systems may be characterized as follows. The established mating system serves primarily one segment of the population: namely, the never-married young. The emerging system serves a much larger and more diverse singles population, including senior citizens, gays, divorced and never-married parents, and some married or separated people, as well as the more traditional group of never-married young adults.

The principal purpose of the established system is to pair off people for lifelong marriage. The principal purpose of the emerging system is to pair off people for intimate relationships that range from marriage to living together to serial monogamy to casual sexual partnerings. The established system links sex, childbearing, and parenthood to marriage, or to the social expectation of marriage. The emerging system treats sex, childbearing, and parenthood as separate from marriage. The established system anchors commitment in a legal contract, a religious covenant, and the exchange of vows in public. The emerging system leaves commitment to individuals' private understandings and mutual consent.

In sum, the established system is a marrying system. Its main purpose has been to support and encourage not-yet-married young men and women to choose and marry a suitable mate, ideally for life. The emerging system is what might be called a "relationships" system. Its purpose is to pair up people of all ages and life stages in intimate relationships of varying levels of duration, commitment, and sexual fidelity.

Society's stake in these two systems is strikingly different. Society has an interest in the formation of lasting marital unions, especially when they include, or are likely to include, dependent children. The social interest in the formation of other kinds of non-child-rearing intimate relationships is not as great. Mainly, society has a stake in ensuring that such partnerships are adult, consensual, and nonviolent. Other than that, the selection of an intimate partner is a matter of private choice and preference, not subject to the interference or involvement of third parties or society at large. Thus, the two systems are radically at odds in their social philosophies: the marriage system is deeply communitarian, while the relationship system is profoundly libertarian.

Because these systems serve different purposes, and because they have been designed for different populations, they also differ in their courtship practices. The courtship practices in the marriage system are designed to help young men and women meet each other in social settings and, through a series of graduated and increasingly public steps, move toward a commitment to marry. The courtship practices in the relationships system are still evolving and hard to discern. However, at least one of the key features of the relationships system—the widespread practice of cohabitation—functions as a form of courtship for some of the marriage-minded young.

In the future, these two systems may be combined or fused in some way. At the moment, however, they coexist, in the same way that radio and television or the New York Stock Exchange and NASDAQ coexist. Yet, unlike these other familiar coexisting entities, the two mating systems have blurry boundaries. It is often hard to know where one leaves off and the other begins. Some singles in society are oriented to the marriage system. Others are situated within the relationships system. Some singles may shift back and forth between the two, depending on their ages, goals, and opportunities.

However, one key member of the singles population doesn't fit easily or comfortably within either: she is the accomplished graduate of the Girl Project who wants to get married and have children. Neither the established nor the emerging system is tailored to her ambitions and desires. The established system, with its pattern of entry into an early marriage, does not fit her new timetable, and the emerging system, with its cycle of short-term, shallow relationships, does not address her desire for marriage or help her find a marriage-minded man in a relationships-oriented singles world.

THE DATING GERONTOCRACY

IN TIMES PAST, THE POPULATION of actively dating singles consisted mainly of the young and not-yet-married. Because marriages were less likely to end in divorce, there were fewer divorced singles than there are today. Widows and widowers made up a larger proportion of the singles population back then, but many were not actively dating. Gays and lesbians were closeted or part of an underground dating scene.

Today, the dating population has changed. It is no longer defined by, or limited to, the young and never married. For one reason, it has gotten older. This is because the American population as a whole is older. The median age of the nation's population has risen to 35.3, the highest in our history. For another reason, the percentage of adults who are single is larger and not limited to people at the very young or very old end of the age spectrum. People are living longer, spending more time as singles before they enter marriage for the first time, and remaining single longer in between and after marriages. They are also choosing to live together rather than to marry. Consequently, as a proportion of the adult life span, single life is getting longer and married life is getting shorter.[4] Indeed, according to one recent study, the proportion of life spent as a single person now exceeds that spent in continuous (undisrupted by legal separation or divorce) marriage. In 1995, men spent slightly more than 45 percent of their life in such a marriage, a decline from 58.4 percent in 1970. For women, the corresponding percentage was 41.2 percent in 1995, compared to 50.5 percent in 1970.[5]

However, though singles may be older, they are not too old for love. The widowed are healthier than they once were, and the elderly are sexier than they once were thanks to Viagra and hormone replacement therapies. Thus, single seniors are more likely to be part of a dating population today. Dating websites such as www.thirdage.com and www.silvermatchmaker.com testify to the growing population of dating seniors. At least one Boston proprietor of a 15-year-old dating service is also seeing signs of this trend. As Mark Goodman, co-owner of the Post Club and veteran matchmaker, told the *Boston Globe*, there's been a ten-year increase in the ages of people whom they can expect to match. "Years ago, if a 50-year-old woman walked in the door, we would shudder. Now that's probably gone to 60."[6]

At the same time that the population of dating singles has gotten grayer, it has also gotten more diverse. In addition to the never-married young, it includes divorced men and women, single parents, and widowed senior citizens. Gays and lesbians of all ages have now joined the above-ground dating population. The broadening in the composition and age of the dating population is a far-reaching, if not yet fully appreciated, social and cultural development. Youth has long been identified as the season of love. In Shakespeare's famous seven ages of man soliloquy, the lover, "sighing like a furnace, with woeful ballad to his mistress' eyebrow," is clearly an adolescent, who appears after the child and schoolboy in the chronological sequence of the seven ages. In modern times, social scientists have also identified love as the special prerogative and challenge of the young. For example, one eminent sociologist, writing in the mid-20th century, characterized romantic love as a practice of adolescent "youngsters," supervised and controlled by parents who threaten, cajole, wheedle, bribe, and persuade their children to "go with the right people" during their childhood love play and later courtship phases.[7] Similarly, 20th century social psychologist Erik Erikson famously identified the formation of romantic love attachments as the defining developmental task for young people.

Because romantic courtship has traditionally been the special prerogative and province of the young, special indulgences and privileges have been granted to young lovers. They can preen and parade, kiss passionately in public, engrave their lovers' names in graffiti on walls or tattoos on their own bodies, obsessively replay songs or create mix tapes to memorialize their love, and they are regarded permissively as crazy kids in love. On the other hand, such love-struck behavior among adults has customarily been considered unseemly. In the literary tradition, lovers past the prime years for mating are often portrayed as faintly ridiculous and their courtships as parodies or comic foils to the passionate romantic pursuits of the young.

Like romantic courtship, marriage used to hold special significance for the young. Until recently, it functioned as a rite of passage into adulthood itself. Getting married meant growing up. Wedding customs reflected the importance of this rite of passage by drawing a sharp distinction between first marriages and subsequent marriages. The first marriage was a great family, social, and religious celebration. Wedding ceremonies of older couples, and especially those who were marrying for the second time, were expected to be quiet and more private affairs. And this was not a feature just of Western marriage. Universally, first marriages are weighted with larger meaning and social significance than later marriages. Among polygymous peoples, moreover, the "first marriage privilege" extends to wives: the first wife has prerogatives over subsequent wives, including the right to be buried next to the husband.[8] (This tradition has not carried over into the practice of serial monogamy in contemporary society, however.)

The emerging relationships system, geared to the growing population of older singles and to those seeking a second or third chance at love, departs from the tradition of youthful courtship. It endows everyone with romantic privileges once reserved for the never-married young. Indeed, its optimistic assumption is that love is not just for the young; it can happen to anyone, at anytime, at any stage in the adult life course. The "Vows" column in the Sunday *New York Times* routinely reports on the amusing, high-concept weddings of aging boomers. In one such nuptial, the 40-something bridegroom, resplendent in a neon-orange silk suit, "played the clarinet as his 40-year-old bride arrived, by freight elevator, in a short vintage white dress, gold pointy high heels, and an organza headpiece the size of a beach ball."[9] Clearly, the understated ceremony for older couples is going the way of the pay telephone.

Another memorable "Vows" column featured the irresistibly charming wedding story of a couple in their 80s who had weathered all the storms of life, including the illness and death of a spouse—and found love again. The bride is vigorous and intellectually vibrant, and hers isn't the rocking chair kind of love. As an admiring caterer told the *Times* columnist: ". . . to see someone marrying the love of her life—this swarthy, sexy-looking, 80-something man—it's really cool."[10]

As yet another cultural sign of this trend, consider the magazine *More*. Designed for aging baby boom women, it contains articles on implant replacement, estrogen replacement, hip replacement, and husband replacement. One of its regular themes is dating relationships, and, in this respect, it is nearly indistinguishable from *Glamour* or *Jane*. One story has a 54-year-old woman spending a week with 20-somethings to see how they live, work, contracept, and exercise.[11] In another, four single 40-something men compare photographs of eight women, ages 28 to 56, to determine whether they prefer youth or maturity. The male consensus is that older is better. The youngest woman gets the worst ratings: she "looks like she'd beat me up," one man comments. The oldest woman, on the other hand, is judged "serious, passionate, and trustworthy," according to another male reviewer.[12] And almost every issue of the magazine includes a story on the "joys of late-in-life love."

THE LADDER OF COMMITMENT

ROMANTIC COURTSHIP IS A PROCESS of mate selection closely connected to marriage. As it has been elaborated and codified in social practice over the ages, it is organized as a linear progression, or ladder, toward marital commitment. In rough order, this ladder begins with some form of mixed-company socializing or casual dating. The next rung is dedicated to pairing off as a couple in an exclusive romantic relationship. After some time together as a couple, the further step up the ladder comes with the mutual decision to marry and then the public announcement of a formal engagement. The progress of the courtship culminates at the top rung of the ladder in the social celebration, and often religious ceremony, of the wedding itself. Each step becomes progressively more public. Each rung has greater institutional recognition and social support. Each level moves the couple higher up the ladder toward marital commitment.

A boyfriend's obligations have been clearly defined by this ladder of commitment: his role is to take romantic initiative at every step in the dating relationship. He has to strike up a conversation, make a phone call, pay for a date, and win the affections of his girlfriend first, and then, gain the approval of her family and friends. The crucial male romantic initiative is the marriage proposal. Once a man is secure in his girlfriend's affections and reasonably confident of her likely consideration, or consent, to marriage, his responsibility is to propose marriage and present her with a tangible symbol of his commitment, usually an engagement ring. This tradition has many variations, of course, and the proposal often evolves slowly as a mutual understanding rather than erupting as a "pop the question" surprise. However, the romantic responsibility exists, not even so much for the sake of propriety or tradition, as much as for the sake of a young woman's feelings of being chosen and special above all others.

In this ladder, each rung also has been surrounded by symbols and rituals of commitment, especially as couples progress toward marriage. Rings and engagements are important, because they enable couples who are past the stage of infatuation to have a shared and unambiguous understanding of their relationship. Moreover, they are public, so they announce this intention to the larger social world. They bring third parties—notably family, close friends, and social acquaintances—into the relationship as sources of advice, support, and feedback. This is especially important in a mating system where the choice of a mate is made freely, mutually, and independently by the couple themselves. Third parties can support, advise, and sometimes offer cautions before the couple reaches the altar. Moreover, such courtship practices are designed to translate the subjective state of being in love into objective expressions of commitment. In this way, they reduce the chances for confusion, misrepresentation, or ambiguity about the nature and future purpose of the romance.

Of course, the symbolic representations of commitment are not enough to guarantee mutual understanding, much less a marriage made in heaven. Romantic relationships are notoriously susceptible to deliberate deception, accidental miscommunication, and wishful thinking. Nevertheless, these rituals provide objective and commonly recognized measures of "where the relationship is headed," so everyone is on the same page.

In the marriage system, there have been two formally recognized ways to get off the ladder of commitment. One is the broken engagement, and the other is the dissolution of marriage. Both forms of breakups are surrounded by social rules, and the breakup of a marriage is, of course, subject to the legal regulation of the state through the institution of divorce. As with the levels of commitment, the levels of "un-commitment" are placed in the context of their relationship to marriage. Thus, a broken engagement is far less serious than a broken marriage. Indeed, since one of the purposes of betrothal in a marrying system is to test commitment to marriage, a broken engagement, however regrettable or embarrassing, traditionally has been treated as protective of marriage. Couples who broke off an engagement could start over again with a clean social slate; though a broken engagement could be disruptive and heartbreaking, it was usually treated as wise and "for the best." In her *Book of Common Sense Etiquette* (1962), Eleanor Roosevelt nicely summed up the social rule: "better a broken engagement than an unhappy period of marriage terminated by divorce."[13]

In the ladder of un-commitment, a boyfriend has the fewest claims on social sympathy. His status is highly probationary, and he can be dropped or leave the relationship at will. A fiancé has been accepted and partially admitted into the circle of family and close friends. His status can still be revoked, but with greater social repercussions. A spouse has the full legal, social, and religious standing accorded through the institution of marriage. Breaking up with a spouse requires legal action and imposes legal and social costs, as well as personal pain.

This system of selecting a mate for marriage has hardly been flawless. Indeed, if the divorce statistics of the '70s and '80s can be taken as a measure of the effectiveness of romantic courtship during the '50s and '60s, then one would have to conclude that it has had a fairly dismal record of success in helping people choose a suitable marriage partner. But that aside, the chief problem with this system of romantic courtship is that it barely exists for the new single woman. As we shall see, it disappeared from the college campus before she even arrived. Moreover, this system of romantic courtship was designed for women who courted and married at a young age, often in their teens or early 20s, not for women who are likely to court and marry at an older age.

THE RELATIONSHIPS CYCLE

THE EMERGING RELATIONSHIPS system has a structure that is different from the romantic courtship and marriage system. It is not a ladder leading toward lifelong marriage, but a series of relationships that form and break up. This cycle can extend throughout the life course. Since contemporary marriage is highly vulnerable to divorce, it is now becoming part of the cycle. Today, first marriages that end in divorce last seven to eight years, on average.[14] Second marriages are more likely than first marriages to end in divorce, and those that do, last for a shorter time before they break up.[15] Indeed, in a relationships cycle, first marriages are *less* important and socially significant than subsequent marriages. Some now refer to first marriages as "icebreaker" marriages, or, as author Pamela Paul brands them in her recent book, "starter marriages." [16]

The relationships system has no necessary connection to marriage. The status and prerogatives of a romantic partner are not defined by a ladder leading to marriage commitment. He can hold any one of several possible statuses: sex buddy, boyfriend, live-in lover, fiancé, or husband. Indeed, the words "partner" and "relationship" deliberately blur any such distinctions. And for many intimate partnerships, little public or social support is required. Third parties need not be involved. All that is needed for a couple to be "in a relationship" is mutual consent.

The relationships system, with its cyclical pattern, treats breakups as inevitable and commonplace events. To be sure, they can be personally painful, but they are a socially necessary part of the creative destruction that goes along with the dynamism of the relationships cycle. Society's challenge is to manage this form of creative destruction so as to minimize disorder, gender conflict, and couple violence. Thus, the relationships system attaches great importance to coming up with better measures for the management of breakups and for the intimate diplomacy of renegotiating relationships with friends, family, and, especially, the children of a former partner. A recent spate of popular self-help books with such titles as *Dumped!; The Complete Idiot's Guide to Handling a Breakup; Exorcising Your Ex;* and *The Heartbreak Handbook* is a sign of this new emphasis on breakup management.

Still, despite these efforts, it is not always easy to achieve gender comity. For one thing, a society of more informal and easily dissoluble intimate unions is a society where there is likely to be persistent male aggression against women—for crimes of violence against women are rooted in male possessiveness and jealousy. Women are at greatest risk for violence when they seek to leave a relationship. For another, the cycle of relationships takes an emotional toll. There are emotional costs associated with the breakups, even when the relationships are short or casual or "just about sex." Despite the freedoms of the sexual revolution, women are still more likely than men to invest sexual partnerships with emotional "meaning," and to confuse sex with genuine affection and even the promise of a future together. From their experience of the "first time" onward, the research suggests, women want sex to "mean" something. They look for affection, tenderness, and commitment in their relationships. The nation's most comprehensive sex survey reports that 48 percent of women have intercourse for the first time out of "affection for their partner," compared to only 25 percent of men.[17] Moreover, for women more than men, sexual coupling is strongly linked to their ideas about "social couplehood." They tend to envision their sexual partnerings as precursors to more socially embedded and emotionally enmeshed relationships.

The problem is that these expectations are often disappointed. And with each betrayal and breakup, the emotional costs mount. The more sex partners, the more breakups, and the greater exposure to emotional bruises such as sadness, loss, anger, and resentment, as well as the accumulation of bitter feelings and cynicism about men in general. As a result, much of the distinctive psychological landscape of the relationships system has a roller coaster feel to it: sexual highs followed by emotional lows. In the aftermath of a brief, intense, exhilarating romance that went bad, a West Coast woman comments on the emotional letdown: "I've allowed this relationship to eat up about two months of my time now. What did I get in those two months? Two dates, one long phone call, some sex I'm not even sure I wanted, and a lot of heartache."

THE DEATH OF COLLEGE COURTSHIP

FOR MUCH OF THE LAST CENTURY, youthful courtship was organized around schooling. Young adults conducted their social life in or around the school campus; they dated classmates or friends of classmates; and they often found the person they would eventually marry among the school population of peers. Moreover, the timing of marriage was closely linked to the completion of schooling. So men and women in their late teens and early 20s frequently began to think about choosing a marriage partner while they were in school.

During most of the 20th century, as more women went to college, and as more colleges became coeducational, the residential college setting became ever more important as a place for a woman to meet the person she would likely marry. By the mid-20th century, as the age of marriage dropped to barely 20, college was seen as a prime marriage market for those who went on to higher education. It brought together a population of never-married men and women who tended to be closely matched in age and educational attainment.

Nowhere in nature was one likely to find such a geographically localized, densely concentrated group of never-married young singles who shared similar backgrounds and aspirations. The student population created through the college admissions process was as artificial and, in those days, as monochromatic as Astroturf. Similarly, the sex ratio was artificially skewed toward a surplus of males. (In nature, slightly more females are born than males.) For most of the 20th century, men outnumbered women on college campuses.

Campus social life was built around coed socializing and dating, usually with some expectation that the social activities would lead to finding a marriage partner. Since men and women lived in separate, same-sex residences, usually on campus, they didn't have regular opportunities to have meals, casual conversations, dorm encounters, or hanging-out time after class or on weekends. Consequently, opportunities for coed socializing outside of class had to be more organized than they are today. Much of the social life of the campus was devoted to bringing men and women together for dances, parties, and sports events and to pairing people off into couples, through such practices as pinning ceremonies. Single-sex schools had their own version of coupling up. Women's colleges often "paired off" with nearby men's colleges. In the late '50s, for example, Radcliffe's student handbook assured its women that they would find "no scarcity of men" in Cambridge.[18] Many college women in the '50s and early '60s expected to be engaged, or at least coupled up, by the end of the senior year. Sex was part of the college dating culture, but it was usually linked to future plans for marriage. Engaged couples were two to three times more likely to have sex than people who were simply dating casually, according to one study of campus romance.[19]

After the mid-1960s, however, this college courtship system began to fall apart. The sexual revolution, the women's movement, the birth control pill, and the countercultural revolt against nuclear family life all contributed to its collapse. By the mid-1980s, the highly organized campus courtship system that had flourished for the first two-thirds of the century had lost its appeal and coherence. "Dating was probably never fun," a 1986 article in the now defunct *Mademoiselle* magazine proclaimed, "but it wasn't navigating shark-infested waters either."[20] In the late 1990s, a pair of Columbia University researchers conducted a large-scale study of college student life based on a survey of more than 9,000 students from 586 colleges and universities and on extensive interviews with college administrators and student leaders. They concluded that "traditional dating is largely dead on college campuses. At institutions all around the country, students told us . . . 'there is no such thing as dating here.'"[21]

In place of the college courtship system, a more collective and comradely pattern of socializing has emerged. The Columbia researchers characterize it as group dating combined with hooking up for casual sex. Friends socialize in unpartnered packs, sometimes with a tightly bonded couple in their midst. Indeed, for collegians today, the "family of friends," a siblinglike group of men and women, provides a principal source of emotional security and attachment. A generation that grew up dealing with Mom and Dad's divorce looks for safety and comfort not in the couple relationship, but in the solidarity of sibs.

Romantic love, the state of affection between sex and friendship, has largely been leached out of college relationships. Indeed, the contemporary pattern of casual sex combined with group friendship offers protection from deeper involvement and intimacy associated with romantic love. A group of Wellesley students, interviewed by the

Columbia researchers, claimed that their inner struggle was to deal with the conflict between their political agenda—getting ahead and therefore feeling more anti-male—and their personal agenda, which was to build a heterosexual relationship. The easiest way to resolve this tension, the Columbia study concludes, is for such women to "squeeze romance and emotion from sexual relationships."[22] According to a psychologist who has counseled students at the University of Chicago, asexual couplings are also common. Gen-X men and women may share beds without ever having sex, or they may start out in a sexual relationship and then shift to a comfy, "friendly ex" living-together arrangement. Lesbians have passionate romantic love, she says, but it is increasingly rare to find it between college men and women.

Undoubtedly, this new form of campus socializing also reflects the new timetable for women's lives. Very few women (or men) go off to college today with the thought, much less the expectation, of finding a future spouse during their undergraduate years. Group dating provides one way to enjoy friendships, including some casual sex, while avoiding the kind of intense emotional involvement that might take too much time away from personal and career pursuits or lead into a too-early commitment. And, indeed, according to some of the women I interviewed, it is simply too stressful and distracting to have a heavy romantic involvement during college.

VARIETIES OF COHABITATION

JUST AS MARRIAGE IS THE signature union of the established system, cohabitation is the signature union of the emerging relationships system. Over the past four decades, it has moved from the seedy margins of the society to the respectable mainstream. Between 1960 and 2000, the number of opposite-sex unmarried couples in America increased from under 500,000 to 4.9 million. Correspondingly, there's been a shift in social attitudes toward cohabitation. Its ratings on the social approval scale have gone from widespread condemnation to majority approval. According to a survey by the Gallup Organization, more than half of Americans today (52 percent) see living together as a morally acceptable lifestyle.[23]

Cohabitation is especially popular among young adults. It has now replaced marriage as the first living-together union for the majority of young women. More than half of unmarried women between the ages of 25 and 39 have lived with a partner, and approximately a quarter of unmarried women in this age category are currently living with a partner.[24] However, cohabiting unions are not all the same. In fact, cohabitation is an intimate opposite-sex partnership that embraces a variety of purposes and commitment levels. There are at least six different types of opposite-sex cohabiting unions, and four that are particularly common among young singles.[25]

One type is explicitly and deliberately non-nuptial. The couple has decided to live together as an alternative to marriage. These relationships are essentially marriages for people who don't believe in the institution of marriage. In Scandinavia, where this kind of cohabiting union is prevalent, it carries virtually all of the social benefits of marriage. Moreover, in Scandinavian countries, as well as in other European nations, such non-nuptial cohabitations typically are long lasting, stable, and often include children. In most respects, they are indistinguishable from marriage. However, in the United States, the Scandinavian-type cohabitation is fairly rare. Here, most cohabiting unions are short-lived; more than half lead into marriage and most of the others fail to survive beyond the five-year mark. Only about 10 percent of cohabiting partnerships last for five years or more.[26]

Another type of cohabiting union is prenuptial. Couples have the "ring and the wedding date," and their living-together arrangement is part of the engagement process. Indeed, they may be living together so that they can fix up the house they will eventually live in as a married couple, or so that they don't have to rent on a short-term basis before the wedding, or so that they can spend time together after work planning for the wedding. (Couples are more likely to plan and pay for their weddings than in the past, when parents ran the show.)

In the first two types, the couples have already chosen each other and are committed to a future together. In the third type, they have not. This is the opportunistic cohabiting union. Couples move in together for reasons that have to do with current circumstances rather than future plans. Indeed, the absence of any kind of future orientation is the hallmark of these partnerships. Some form because couples want to share expenses, especially when they are working in cities with astronomically high living costs: according to this logic, "since we're together all the time anyway, why pay two rents?" Sometimes people move in together because one of them has no other place to live.

Yet another reason for opportunistic cohabitation is simply that it presents an alternative to living alone. Loneliness can be a powerful rationale for sharing a place. And cohabitation also works as part of a life-course strategy to put off marriage until personal and career goals are accomplished. Living together provides some of the sexual and domestic comforts, as well as economies of scale, of marriage without requiring anyone to compromise or coordinate their future plans.

Not surprisingly, many of these cohabiting unions are pre-programmed to self-destruct. One or both of the individuals go into the relationship with the view that "if this doesn't work out, we will break up." Such understandings are perfectly in accord with the new mating cycle and its more informal, private, "mutually consenting but free to leave" terms. And they work fine as long as both individuals share exactly the same level of commitment and emotional investment in the relationship.

The fourth type of living-together union is cohabitation-as-courtship. In this arrangement, the couple may be considering the possibility of eventual marriage. They want to try out marriage by living together first. Such testing for marital compatibility is hardly new. It is one of the classic features of romantic courtship, but today it is taking the contemporary form of living together.[27]

There are several reasons why cohabitation is becoming such an important part of courtship. First of all, people often become passionately involved sexually before they know each other very well. After they become sexually intimate, they still have to become familiar with their partner's character, interests, habits, and daily routines. By living together, they believe, they can gather valuable and otherwise unobtainable information about a prospective spouse's compatibility for marriage. Moreover, as some women have explained to me, you can't get a realistic picture of a partner based on the idealized image he puts forward on a date or the good sex you have together. You want to see your boyfriend in the morning, as he rolls out of bed, unshaven, unshowered, and uncaffeinated. If you still love him in his unsexy morning state, they say, then it's likely you will love him as a husband.

Second, cohabitation-as-courtship is a way to deal with the time crunch in working singles' lives. When romantic courtship occurred during the college years, it could unfold in a leisurely way and in a convenient place. Today, romantic pursuits have to be squeezed into the routines and schedule of a work life. Young adults who are living in cities, attending graduate or professional school, or working full time have limited time to look for suitable partners to date. Some personal ad placers now confine their search to a limited geographic radius, because they can't afford to spend a lot of time in long commutes on congested expressways.[28] And then, when they do find a romantic partner, their work schedules are often at odds. Living together ensures time together on a regular basis and avoids the complicated logistics and travel time associated with formal dating. As one young woman told me, "my boyfriend and I are on very different work schedules—he's in medical school, and I work in television. If we didn't live together, we would never see each other."

And finally, cohabitation-as-courtship is commonly viewed as a way of preventing divorce. In fact, no good social science evidence exists to support the popular view that cohabitation improves the chances for a long-lasting marriage, and some evidence suggests that living together before marriage may increase the divorce risk for cohabiting couples if they eventually marry. Yet for today's young adults who grew up in the midst of the divorce revolution and want to avoid divorce in their own lives, this is a common belief and compelling rationale for cohabitation. Sixty-two percent of men and women ages 20 to 29 agree that living together with someone before marriage is a good way to avoid an eventual divorce, and 43 percent agree that they would only marry someone if he or she agreed to live together first. And, of course, it's true that if cohabiting couples find out that they are not suited for marriage, they can split up rather than end up with an unhappy marriage or an eventual divorce.

THE FEMALE PROPOSAL

IN THE RELATIONSHIPS SYSTEM, the responsibility for taking romantic initiative doesn't fall as heavily on men. Today, the woman is free to make the first phone call, to suggest a date, and to propose sex. This shift extends to what used to be the classic male initiative: a marriage proposal. Of course, men still propose marriage, but they are not obliged to do so. Instead, the burden of responsibility for proposing marriage rests with the individual who wants the commitment. Very often, it's the woman. In the emerging relationships system, the classic male proposal "Will you marry me?" has given way to the female query: "Where is this relationship headed?" Indeed, one of the popularly debated "relationship issues" among women today is "when should I bring up the question of marriage?"

As with any marriage proposal, the female proposal is fraught with uncertainty and risk. If he doesn't want to "move forward" to a higher level of commitment, and she does, then she may have to face up to the implications and end the relationship. Taking the initiative to leave can often be harder than summoning the resolve to stay. And sometimes when she proposes, she gets no firm answer either way. Tragically, for one New York woman, the unresolved question of marriage never got a chance to be resolved. According to a "love story" reported in the *Wall Street Journal*, this 42-year-old professional woman had lived together happily with her boyfriend for eight years. She had grown up in a warm, happy household and wanted to get married, but he had been scarred by his parents' divorce, and was skittish about marriage. As the *Journal* reporter tells us: One night, as the couple was sitting on the couch eating mango sorbet, she turned to her guy and asked, "Bob, why won't you just marry me?" According to the story, "he put his head on her lap and didn't answer." (My translation: a resounding "not ready.") The next day she went off as usual to her job as director of research at Fiduciary Trust Company in Tower Two of the World Trade Center, and that was the last time he saw her. "Now I'd marry her in a second," he said to the *Journal* reporter.[29]

PRIVILEGED IN LIFE, UNDERPRIVILEGED IN LOVE

FOR MANY PEOPLE, THE EMERGING mating system offers clear advantages over the established one. It is more diverse, more inclusive, and offers a cafeteria selection of intimate arrangements. There are more options and choices and far less social stigma attached to any one of the nontraditional intimate partnerships. The marriage system has a history of moralizing about sex and marriage: it condemned premarital sex for women, frowned on divorce, placed same-sex and living-together relationships beyond the social pale, and stigmatized unwed motherhood. The relationship system, however, imposes no such moral judgments. Singles can tailor their relationships according to their own devices and desires, without fear of social or moral disapproval and without the social regulation that existed in the marriage system. This kind of flexible, egalitarian, nonjudgmental approach to the conduct of intimate life is especially advantageous for older and previously married singles, as well as for gays and lesbians, who have been legally excluded from the marriage system altogether.

Moreover, as it turns out, the new system is nicely adapted to men's sexual and romantic self-interests, and especially to the interests of well-educated and affluent men. For generations, if not eons, the goal of young men has been to get nice young women to go to bed with them. Hugh Hefner built an entertainment empire based on the idea that college men needed advice on how to seduce nice college women. However, in the past, these men faced obstacles in persuading a nice girl to have sex without making special efforts to romance her, to prove themselves worthy, and to earn her affections. Today, single guys don't have as much need for advice on how to get a college girl into bed. They can count on a pool of attractive peer women who are willing to sleep with them, compete over them, take care of them, spend money on them, and make no big demands of them. And many men now believe that they have no reciprocal responsibility to her beyond her orgasm, if that.

Moreover, living together is a great deal for a guy who wants to keep his options open as long as possible. He can gain many of the advantages of marriage, without throwing his cap over the wall. He doesn't have to venture anything, risk anything, or commit to anything. He does not have to meet, much less, pass muster with parents, family members, or friends. And he doesn't even have to make a proposal to live together: all he has to do is spend a lot of time at her place, let his clothes, sports gear, and toiletries accumulate, and then wonder out loud whether it makes sense to pay two rents. And of course, when it's over, he can leave it to her to pack up his stuff. Indeed, the benefits of cohabitation for men help to explain why there is no courtship crisis for high achieving young men.

The new single woman also enjoys some of the advantages and freedoms of the relationships system in her early adult years. But as she approaches the time in her life when she is interested in finding a life mate, some of these advantages diminish. Indeed, she is likely to discover that she is entering new, unfamiliar, and often unfriendly terrain. This is why the Chick Lit portrait of the girl without a guide, groping blindly through uncharted and difficult terrain, is apt. She's embarked on an extreme adventure, full of sheer drop-offs, blind alleys, and lonesome gulches.

Perhaps the most telling sign of a loss of privilege is the lack of social sympathy for her ambition to marry. Sex and relationships are socially acceptable ways for a Girl Project graduate to meet her intimacy needs. But there is something in the new single woman's professed desire for marriage, as well as in her manifest frustration in her search for a husband, that runs against the official story of women's social progress.

Young educated women are supposed to stand on their own two feet, not feel weak in the knees; they're supposed to enjoy sex for fun, not whine about commitment; they're supposed to hold up the banner of "Girls Rule," not join the ranks of Rules Girls. If they express a desire for marriage, they've somehow violated the social compact. After all, through the Girl Project, the society has encouraged and invested in their independence from marriage, and somehow it seems like a betrayal for women to complain about their unfulfilled desires for marriage and a family. Compared to the broad social support for their success in school and work, there is scant sympathy for their efforts to be successful in finding lasting love.

A case in point: In 1998, the *Boston Globe* ran a front-page, seven-day series on the real-life romantic adventures of a single woman named Leslie Boorse.[30] At the time, it seemed like an inspired idea. After all, Boston is full of professional young singles, and it was then the sitcom home to television's most famous romantic head case, Ally McBeal. Why not take a look at a real woman who fit the McBeal profile? Enter Leslie Boorse, "a Boston woman of the '90s, 5'7"?, 124 pounds, loose dirty-blond curls, and round blue eyes, a face the shape of a heart and a heart that had been broken once." Unattached and just turned 30, Leslie has put marriage at the top of her list of things to accomplish in the coming year. A *Globe* reporter trails her around as she dates and breaks up with two guys and then meets Ross, a medical student soon to graduate from Columbia University's Medical School. By installment seven of the series, Leslie has decided to move to New York to live with Ross and to work in the Manhattan office of her high tech company. The series ends with Leslie's tentative exploration of her future with Ross: "I said something to him the other night," she tells the reporter in this final installment. "You know, most couples have named their children and talked about what sort of house they want." Ross laughed. "Are you setting me up for something?"[31]

The reader reaction to this serialized story of a young woman's quest for a marriage mate was surprisingly hostile. In a follow-up to the story, the *Globe* ombudsman reported that "in more than 200 responses . . . *Globe* readers denounced the series by a margin of 40 to 1 and, worse, expressed their disapproval in language that made clear the series had left them bewildered, exasperated, even resentful: "Stupid." "Seven parts, but it felt like seven years." "As if this drivel isn't bad enough in Living, now it's spreading like a disease throughout the paper." As is customary, the *Globe* editors offered a defense of the story. Explained managing editor Greg Moore: "She was grappling with issues: turning 30, looking for love, trying to be honest. Those are issues for young and old." But the ombudsman sided with the *Globe*'s fuming readers. He wrote: "With all the issues facing women, to reduce their conflicts and challenges, as this series did, to a self-absorbed 30-year-old's preoccupation with dating is one more example of the shrinking of women to pathetic stereotypes. Grade: D."[32]

We've come a long way from the time when the crowning achievement in a woman's life was her youthful marriage. And many would agree that this represents progress for women. But when did the search for someone to marry become self-absorbed and pathetic? This absence of social sympathy for women's ambitions to marry is all the more striking because the social world has cared so deeply about virtually every other aspect of these privileged young women's inner and outer lives. And it has done so much to coach and instruct women on their sexuality, on the pursuit of sexual pleasure, and the proper conduct of their sex lives. The achievement of a good marriage is the one area of life where the most privileged, accomplished, and high achieving young women in society face a loss of support and sympathy for their ambitions and where the social expectations are for disappointment and failure, not success. As one young woman told me, "Society sucks all the hope out of us."

SHOULD WE LIVE TOGETHER?

IF A CORPS OF MISCHIEVOUS SOCIAL engineers had deliberately set out to create confusion and uncertainty in the new single woman's search for love, they couldn't have come up with a more effective device than cohabitation-as-courtship. Currently, cohabitation is a highly ambiguous kind of arrangement. It can mean one thing at one stage of life and another thing at another stage. It can be a time-efficient way to combine love with a busy working life or a time-wasting way to pour love into a relationship that doesn't work. Since more than half of all cohabiting unions lead into marriage, and most of the rest lead to a breakup within a few years, a living-together relationship can have exactly opposite outcomes.[1] It can be a path to the altar or a path in the other direction.

To be sure, the same could be said of traditional romantic courtship. The purpose of romantic courtship is designed to test for mutual compatibility and to explore the possibility of a long-term commitment. In any such matchmaking process, there is bound to be uncertainty about the outcome, inefficiencies of time, and some relationships that don't (and often shouldn't) make it to the altar.

However, a key difference between traditional courtship and cohabitation-as-courtship is that the earlier approach to mate selection was surrounded by formal rules and social rituals that helped reduce some of the uncertainties about the future course of the relationship. There was also a received body of experience, opinion, and wisdom on the conduct of romantic courtship. There were graduated steps that marked the progress, or lack of progress, in the courtship process. And, of course, when courtship led to the decision to form a marital union, there were public announcements, social celebrations, and eventually a legal contract and the exchange of public vows.

At the present, there is nothing comparable for cohabitation-as-courtship. It has become a mainstream practice only recently, and it has not yet given rise to a clear and widely shared set of rules and rituals. (There is a growing body of legal opinion and legislation on domestic partnerships, of course, but this has little to do with the courtship function of contemporary cohabitation.) Moreover, because cohabitation conflates courtship and a living-together union, there is nothing that formally marks the entry into a cohabiting partnership. A couple's decision to cohabit is made privately. Sometimes this decision is thoughtful and purposeful, but very often it is made casually.

People can slide into living together, without any serious discussion or mutual understanding as to its meaning, purpose, or likely duration, and without much preparation, other than renting the U-Haul. As a consequence, cohabitation-as-courtship can contribute to confusion, misunderstanding, miscommunication, and faulty assumptions. It is easy for a couple to decide to live together and, at the same time, harbor very different expectations for the relationship.

In the absence of any widely shared rules, rituals, or received bodies of experience and teaching, it is necessary for individual women to adopt their own policy and to make their own judgments on when and why to cohabit. For a younger woman, who is not yet ready to marry, a cohabiting relationship may fit her needs and timetable. Living together offers time efficiencies and economies at this stage in her life. She can integrate love into her work life without giving up her freedom. If she is pursuing a career, or another degree, she has to be ready to go where her opportunities lead. This often means breaking up and moving on. One West Coast lawyer, now in her 30s, recalls a soon-after-college relationship that went on for a year and a half during her 20s. "We were in love," she says, but it "wasn't time for our relationship to be 'it.' He was going in his direction and I was going in mine."

For a woman who is thinking about marriage, however, the advantages of cohabitation can be more equivocal. Time considerations are different. Each year she spends in a cohabiting relationship that doesn't "work out" is one less year available to invest in a successful search for a life partner. And, at this stage of her life, each year counts for a large proportion of her prime time for finding a husband. Also, if she stays too long in a cohabiting relationship, she begins to incur what economists call opportunity costs. While she is waiting for Mr. Not Ready or Mr. Maybe or Mr. Someday to make up his mind, she is missing opportunities to meet other potential partners who may be ready and willing to marry. Early on, she must make a determination of where the relationship is going, how quickly and smoothly it's going to get to a desired goal, and on what terms. If she cannot establish that the relationship will lead to marriage, sooner rather than later, then she must end it, cut her losses, and move on. The trouble is, the ambiguity of cohabitation-as-courtship undermines her ability to make such an assessment and to act on it. It is all too easy for such a woman to think that the relationship is progressing toward future marriage while her partner is content with the status quo.

A CAUTIONARY TALE

EMILY IS A DOCUMENTARY FILM producer with striking hazel eyes, a serene demeanor, and a wry sense of humor. She entered into her first and only cohabiting relationship when she was 30. She met her boyfriend, Sean, at a friend's dinner party. At the time, she had just moved across half the country to a charming college town to find work, and maybe also love. The move gave her a shot of optimism and hope. It meant the beginning of a new life. She saw it as a chance to meet new people, build a career, and lead a more stable, grown-up life.

During her teens and early 20s, Emily had been a free spirit. She had traveled around the country for several years before college, but once she entered college, she became a serious and successful student. She graduated with honors and spent the next few years living and working in Chicago, with time out for a 60-day sojourn in Europe. In the year before her move, she had had three brief (six- to eight-week) relationships. But she had wanted a long-lasting relationship for a long time, and this new chapter in her life might bring an opportunity to get it.

Through a network of friends, she had heard that Sean was smart—he could do the *New York Times* crossword puzzle in a half hour—and a talented artisan. He did both carpentry and custom woodwork. Someone showed her a beautifully crafted table that he had made. She was impressed. She chatted with Sean at dinner and sensed an immediate mutual attraction. In the next few weeks, he pursued her. Emily was flattered by the attention and his unflagging interest. After her past experiences with a string of short-termers, she remembers thinking: "Hey, this guy is sticking around."

They met in January and moved in together in April. In the first flush of infatuation with small town life, Emily had rented a house in the country. Then she had second thoughts. A city girl, she found the nights spooky. She realized how isolated she was. Having Sean in the house was comforting. And, as it happened, he needed a place to stay. He had been living with his brother temporarily while he looked for his own space. It made sense to live together. Emily could feel safer, and Sean could feel more securely sheltered. And Emily appreciated having someone who would split living expenses with her and share the pleasures of a promising new relationship.

The first year they lived together it "felt like a big adventure." Emily liked the way her life was going. She had found work as a producer of documentaries, and she had established a serious relationship with someone she cared for. She also got to meet Sean's parents, an elegant academic couple, who approved of her relationship with their son. Their work situations were less satisfying. Though Emily liked her job, it didn't pay much, and it was hard for Sean to get top dollar as a craftsman. They began to discuss the possibility of moving on, together. Since Sean's skills were portable, they agreed that they should move to a place where Emily could find a good job. So she quietly began a job search.

A few months later, Sean made a visit to his parents to do some work on the rental properties they owned. Days after he left, a television station in the Midwest invited Emily for a job interview. Since Sean was hundreds of miles away, fulfilling a longstanding commitment to his parents, Emily went alone, even though she didn't feel comfortable sizing up a prospective place for them without Sean's presence and participation. Emily did a round of interviews over several days, got a look at a new town, and weighed the terms of the offer. At the same time, she kept trying to call Sean to fill him in. He was hard to reach, however, and when she did manage to get him on the phone, she didn't want to get into a heated discussion about their future with his parents possibly within earshot of his side of the conversation. His one-week visit to his parents stretched into a two-week stay, and, at times, he seemed emotionally distant. But Emily didn't have the breathing space to think much of it at the time. And soon they were back home together with a decision to make: should they use Emily's job offer as their ticket to a new place? Sean said he liked the idea, but wondered how long it would take him to build a new clientele for his work.

At that point, a subtle but significant shift occurred in Emily's thinking about the relationship. She offered to support Sean until he could build his business. This isn't just a loan to a boyfriend, she figured at the time. It could also be an investment in a future husband—though she didn't say this to him. For her, living with Sean now became more than just an end in itself. It became, if only to a degree, a path to marriage. Sean accepted her offer, she accepted the new job, and they quickly packed up and moved.

The year after the move was stressful. Emily's new job had long hours and impossible demands. At first, Sean had little work and no friends. For Emily, however, he was an emotional rock. He listened to her "trouble talk" about her job for hours at a time. He encouraged, soothed, and strategized with her. Two years after the move, they decided to buy a house together. Although Sean worked only sporadically, he managed to put up the bulk of the down payment, thanks to some help from his parents. He knew what to look for in a house, so they got a good buy. The house had a workshop for him, and he had time to make improvements in the house when he wasn't working. He also found a business partner who helped him purchase a sawmill. Sean's business was fully equipped and ready to take off.

Then out of the blue, Emily got a job offer to produce a new nationally syndicated show in a city more than 500 miles away. Of course, the timing was hardly ideal, but the job appeared to be a culmination of Emily's professional aspirations. Why pass up such a great job just because of a house? So the plan was for Sean to stay with his business and capitalize on the infrastructure of a house, workshop, and sawmill. Emily would try the new job to get a taste of the big time and to ward off the possibility of future regrets over an opportunity not taken. Besides, the mortality rate for new shows was high, and she would return if it failed.

Emily's big new job turned out to be a big disappointment. Her boss was unreasonably demanding, the deadline pressure was constant, and the hours were long. Nonetheless, Emily felt she had to hang on for at least six months or risk damaging her professional reputation. Moreover, as her reward for sticking it out, she could look forward to returning to Sean and their house. For the first time in her life, she wanted to get married and start a family, and their new place seemed like the perfect launching pad. An integral part of Emily's picture of their future domestic life was that Sean would become successful enough to support her and a child. She felt she had worked hard for nearly four years to keep them financially afloat and that she deserved a break. Besides, she was growing weary from the effort. Meanwhile, back home, Sean proved to be lost without her. Via long distance, she tried to boost his spirits and bolster his resolve, but finally they decided to sell the house and live together in her new place. After Sean arrived, he managed to hit the ground running. He knew houses, so he got his real estate license and quickly made two sales, even as he found customers for his woodworking. Emily felt she could relax. It was nice to share breadwinning responsibilities more equally. But then her career hit a snag. The show failed. For the first time since she had met Sean, she was out of work. Still, she thought, maybe it was for the best. She was closing in on 35. Now, during her idle days, she would take walks to the park and watch mothers with their children. "I used to think, 'there's a woman whose husband is supporting her' and feel envious because I doubted that Sean was capable of doing that for me and a child." Nonetheless, she felt committed to the relationship and too invested to walk away. She resigned herself to the future prospect of being a working mom, even though that future looked more stressful and tiring than the life she had been leading without children. She told Sean that she felt it was time to think about marriage and children.

The short version of the story is that he bolted. The longer version: almost as soon as Emily raised the subject of marriage, Sean
had a brief affair with a woman who was a guest in a house he was
remodeling. It was a ready-made opportunity for a man who needed
a *casus breakup*. He was the sexy carpenter and she was the bored
guest. He immediately informed Emily that he had fallen in love
with another woman. They sought emergency therapy (three sessions
in three days), but it was too late. He told the counselor he wanted
out. They divided up the household, and Emily kept a small table he
had made. After five years together, their relationship was over.

Since then, Emily has had time to gain some distance and perspective on the "Sean" experience. To her, it had seemed as if their
relationship were progressing naturally to marriage. And there was
ample reason for her to think that they were on a ladder of commitment. They had gone through a long trial period together, including
moves, job changes, and the purchase and sale of a house. They
enjoyed each other sexually and stood by each other emotionally.
Sean had supported her career ambitions, and she had invested time
and money in helping him to establish his business. "I knew that he
was a fixer-upper," she says, "but he contributed too. And I loved
that security, the home life, and the sense of being protected."

At the same time, however, Emily now realizes how far apart they
were in their future goals. She envisioned marriage and children as
the likely and logical next step in the evolution of their relationship,
while Sean saw it as a huge, frightening, and ultimately impossible
leap from dependency into responsibility. But the radical difference
in their expectations and goals never surfaced because they never
had the conversation that would put those expectations on the table.
"Our relationship was focused on work. We were 'into our work' and

our relationship revolved around supporting each other's work ambitions." Though Emily never before gave much thought to marriage vows, she now sees their value. "We never vowed to do anything."

There were signals, she realizes, but she didn't make enough of them at the time. When Sean visited his parents and acted chilly on the phone, that was a signal. He later disclosed in therapy that he had had cold feet. (A job offer elsewhere is often an occasion for a partner to end a relationship.) Ultimately, though, he decided to stay—not so much to affirm the relationship as to put off the breakup. Another time, Emily chipped in heavily for a gift for Sean's sister. A few days later, he said, almost absently, "I signed my name on the card." Emily was miffed that he hadn't included her, but she didn't call him on it.

Emily's story illustrates the downside of cohabitation for the marriage-minded woman. She invested five of her prime marrying years in the relationship. When her relationship ended, she was 35, unpartnered, and no closer to finding a suitable man than when she was 30. In addition, before she could feel the desire and confidence to date again, she had to take a year to recover emotionally. Further, when Emily began to live with Sean, she saw what they had as a "relationship." Along the way, however, her goals changed. She began to aspire to marriage. This changed her view of Sean. In her mind, he moved from a live-in boyfriend to a husband-in-the-works. It would take him awhile to complete the full transformation, she figured, but she was helping him to move in this direction. However, as she discovered, this was not an expectation or goal that Sean shared.

It's certainly easy to see how living with a man can seem like a path into marriage. Cohabiting relationships bear some resemblances to marriage, and more than 50 percent do convert into marriage. But the new practice of cohabitation-as-courtship doesn't unfold as reliably as a marriage-minded woman might expect.

Of course, this is hardly unique to cohabitation. A romantic relationship between a man and woman who live at separate addresses can also go sour. What is unique to the practice of cohabitation-as-courtship, however, is that it has special characteristics that make it hard for a woman *to know or to admit to herself* that it is going sour. So it is important to know what these characteristics are and to be mindful of how easily they can cloud judgment about the actual nature and future of the partnership.

GETTING ENMESHED

COHABITATION IS INTENDED TO preserve an individual's independence in an intimate relationship, and, in some respects, it does exactly that. Recent research indicates that cohabitors behave like side-by-side singles rather than like a married couple. According to social demographer Linda Waite, one of the nation's leading experts on cohabitation, they are more separate than married couples in their friends, their finances, and their family networks. They are also more likely to have another sexual partner, even though they say that they expect their live-in partner to be faithful. Not surprisingly, cohabitors are also less committed to the idea of sexual fidelity even when they are currently faithful to their partner. "In cohabitation, you're not working as a team," says Waite. "You're just sort of together on the bus."[2]

However, at the same time that living-together partners retain their separateness, there are subtler forms of entanglement that can make the relationship risky for a woman who hopes to marry. For one, a woman is likely to get emotionally enmeshed in the relationship. She takes responsibility for the emotional care and tending of an intimate relationship, and this seems to happen whether she is married or cohabiting. She goes out of her way to create a comfortable nest. She takes the lead in keeping track of his dentist appointments, wardrobe decisions, and towel supply. She bonds with his dogs or gets a puppy for them to share. She gets to know his ex-girlfriend, or ex-wife. She helps out with his children when they visit on the weekends or during the summer.

Rebecca, 29, a New Yorker who works as an e-business consultant, played a heroic role in supporting her live-in boyfriend through a major eye surgery. She searched the Internet for medical specialists, met with his doctors, gave him advice about signing a Do Not Resuscitate order (she argued against it, because she didn't want him to feel depressed or scared by the thought of cardiac arrest or brain damage), notified his family and his ex-girlfriend that he had come through the operation, and spent several days in a hotel away from home while he recuperated in the hospital. Women like Rebecca find it emotionally rewarding to make life better for someone they love. Her boyfriend's vision is now restored, and she takes pride in the role she played in his successful recovery. But as women volunteer for care-giving responsibility, they build an emotional stake in the relationship that isn't secured by a commitment of any kind.

A cohabiting woman can also allow her life to become financially enmeshed with his. Even though she may keep her bank account and stocks separate, she can get enmeshed without commingling liquid assets. She can volunteer to help organize and manage his finances. One investment banker, who had been "into" the stock market since girlhood and had a healthy portfolio of her own, was appalled by her boyfriend's careless money management. He earned a lot of money as a consultant, but his income came in spurts. He would get a big check, but he didn't know how to save or invest. So his check melted away almost as soon as he got it. She set him up with a SEP, IRA, and stock investment program, which he may still have as a financial keepsake of their now defunct three-year relationship.

A woman can also become financially enmeshed in an effort to help him "get on his feet" after some kind of financial or employment setback. She may lend him money to help him start a business or pay off a debt. Or, like Emily, she can offer to support him, or perhaps pay the entire rent, until he gets a job or finishes a degree. A common form of financial enmeshment is the purchase of a house. For some couples, buying a house together is a step that comes right before marriage, while for others, it has no necessary connection to marriage. Either way, it means that the couple is financially enmeshed and mutually obligated for as long as they both share the mortgage.

For a woman who wants to marry, therefore, the cohabiting relationship poses a risk. These entanglements make it harder for her to see and act on any signs that the relationship is not going to lead to the desired goal. Instead of conserving her time, she might invest even more time in a stagnating relationship, in an effort to preserve the emotional investment she has already made. Moreover, once she is enmeshed, it is all too tempting to see him as equally enmeshed and dependent on her continued care. Any evidence to the contrary can be ignored, excused, or explained away. Thus, it can come as a shock when a needy boyfriend decides to get his needs fulfilled elsewhere.

But there is a far more fundamental problem. It resides in the very nature of cohabitation itself. Though cohabiting unions can look a lot like marriages, they are very different. In fact, some of the defining characteristics of cohabitation are the exact opposites of the characteristics of marriage. Cohabitation is an agreement reached privately. Marriage is an event celebrated publicly. Cohabitation is based on mutual consent. Marriage is based on a legal contract and, in many cases, on a religious covenant. Cohabitation is entered into informally, even casually. Marriage is entered into with all kinds of formal rituals and ceremonies. Cohabitation is between two adults. Marriage joins together two families. Cohabitation is a nonbinding commitment for an indeterminate period. Marriage sets forth a clear statement as to the nature and expected duration of the commitment.

No one who marries in a state of sobriety can be unclear about what he or she is doing on the wedding day or what he or she is committing to. In a marriage, there are multiple and overlapping ways in which the couple's mutual agreement is enacted, announced, proclaimed, contracted, pledged, and celebrated. This is not the case with cohabitation. Unlike the entry into marriage, the entry into a cohabiting partnership requires nothing more than a change-of-address card. Indeed, it is in the nature of the cohabiting partnership to mean whatever each of the individual partners wants it to mean, and these separate meanings can be wildly different. She can harbor one set of expectations for the relationship, and he can have another.

Thus, though a marriage-minded woman consents to the partnership, she often does so without ever having a conversation about her desires for the future. In fact, the implicit deal is that cohabiting couples don't look very far into the future. They have to see how things work out for the present. Women have been told that talking about marriage is a big turn-off to guys. And of course, it does reek of desperation when a single woman talks incessantly about her younger sister's wedding or her own future wedding plans on a first or second date. But that prohibition against talking about marriage can now extend into a living-together partnership. So cohabitation-as-courtship is a way of trying out marriage without ever talking about it.

When there are disparities in levels of commitment, one scholar has noted, the partner who is less committed has the greater power in the relationship.[3] Moreover, the less committed partner has a stake in keeping understandings about the future as ambiguous and contingent as possible. One common way of underscoring the contingency of cohabitation-as-courtship is to make it an "if, then" deal, as in: "if I get the job or the promotion, then we'll talk marriage," or "if we get the house, then we'll start thinking about marriage." Another way is to mention marriage as a destination, but as one that is still remote. One man kept his live-in girlfriend on hold for six years by telling her that "he was working up to the point of marriage."

According to one study of cohabiting couples, this kind of persistent uncertainty leads to hypervigilance about any shred of information relevant to commitment. There is the tendency to interpret "every event that comes along as commitment enhancing or commitment reducing."[4] But that information is often ambiguous and hard to decipher. In cohabiting partnerships, a vast world of obscure meaning, consisting of incidents, gestures, and casual comments, has to be deconstructed and interpreted with an eye to his future intentions. "What did he really mean when he said 'Let's make this anniversary really "special"?' Could it mean a ring?" In the fog, it is easy to misinterpret. One young woman told me that at the time she started living with her boyfriend, she casually remarked: "Gee, if we keep this up, we might end up getting married." He responded with a "huh," or maybe it was an "uh-hun." She took it as a "*yes*." Three years later, she was devastated when he announced that he wanted to see other women. While she had been thinking about bridesmaids, he had been checking out the babes.

SHE'S THINKING "HUSBAND," HE'S THINKING "BOYFRIEND"

A WOMAN'S VIEW OF THE KIND of commitment represented by cohabitation is often very different from a man's view, as I have learned from one-on-one interviews and focus group discussions with young singles over the past three years. Young women place commitment along a continuum, with intimate relationships reflecting lesser and greater degrees of commitment. Marriage stands at the far end of the commitment continuum, but other partnerships, like cohabitation, can be placed at several intermediate points along the line. What's more, women tend to speak about commitment as if it were evolutionary in its development. They talk about "where the relationship is headed" or "the direction we're going" or "the track we're on." They are continually gauging the degree and direction of commitment in this progression. They are "moving forward toward" greater closeness and commitment or they are stuck in the same rut or they are "moving in the wrong direction."

Because women see commitment as part of an unfolding evolutionary (or devolutionary) process, they are accustomed to assessing their live-in boyfriend's commitment based on a nuanced and complex reading, not only of his deeds, but also of his words (including their inflections), his gestures, his facial expressions—and even his silences. Is he in the same place today as he was yesterday or last month? Have his feelings changed? Women's tendency to read the relationship in evolutionary terms also encourages hopes that their boyfriend is a husband-in-the-works. Through the experience of living together, they believe, he will acquire an aptitude for, and comfort level with, marriage—even if he was scared of commitment going into the relationship.

Young men's view of commitment is more binary. As they see it, commitment is a matter of status, and when it comes to status, there are two choices: not married or married. Unlike women, they don't see shadings of degree; they see differences in kind. To go from the status of "not married" to "married" is not just a small step from where you've been; it is a status-changing leap. And a man doesn't make this leap on the day he moves his stuff into your place, or vice versa. He only makes it on the day that he says "I do." Until he makes that leap, he remains in the "not married" category. Consequently, for men, cohabitation is just one way of being single. Even if he is living with a girlfriend, in his own view, he remains psychologically and even morally free to keep looking.

Because men see marital commitment as a status, they take seriously the formal, legal, and public events, ceremonies, and rituals that mark the change in their status from "not married" to "married." They assign far less weight to the informal, intimate, and private gestures and understandings that serve, for a woman, as benchmarks along the way to marriage. That is one of the reasons for the custom of engagement. Betrothal is not just a ring for her; it's part of the transition to a new status for him. Men who are formally engaged begin to see themselves as married. Similarly, although it is generally assumed that a wedding is an event designed for the bride, it is far more psychologically and socially significant for the groom. It is the event that marks his leap into a new kind of commitment and status.

Given these differences, it is easy to see how a cohabiting relationship can lead to so much misunderstanding and difficulty for a woman who is ready to marry. She is likely to see the decision to live together as part of an investment of time and affection that may pay off in a marriage. Consequently, she takes on some of the nurturing, supportive roles of the wife in the expectation that they are building a mutual stake in future marriage. But her boyfriend may see it as a pay-as-you-go relationship. He takes it one day at a time and figures that the book is balanced at the end of the day. After all, he has taken no formal or legal step to change his status from "not married" to "married." So he has assumed no obligation to her to marry. This is why some cohabiting men are surprised, scared, or mystified when their live-in girlfriend brings up the subject of marriage and why they see talk of marriage as a form of "pressure" to change the terms of the bargain. On the other side, this is why some cohabiting women feel cruelly deceived when their live-in boyfriends balk at the subject of marriage. For her, cohabitation is part of the evolution toward marriage—and she has yet to reach it. For him, cohabitation is the status of being a single guy with a live-in girlfriend—and he's already there.

WHY COHABITATION FAVORS MEN

JUST AS COHABITATION-AS-COURTSHIP can be a bad bargain for a marriage-minded woman, it can be a good deal for a man. He can get the benefits of a wife without shouldering the reciprocal obligations of a husband. Her investment of time, effort, and support subsidizes his domestic comfort, his physical health, and his emotional well-being. Unlike other forms of live-in help, moreover, she is sexually available and works for free.

Men are figuring this out. In a study of young single men conducted by the National Marriage Project, a number of them expressed the view that cohabitation is a way to get the benefits of marriage without exposing themselves to the financial toll of divorce, should the relationship break up. They were acutely aware of the cost of divorce to a man, especially if he lives in a so-called community property state, where the law assigns half of marital assets to the wife. For such men, living with a woman is financially far less risky and domestically just as comfy as a marriage.[5]

In fact, for some men, cohabitation may fit into a revolving-door pattern of mother-girlfriend caregiving. In the past, it was a young woman who was a dependent, first in her father's and then in her husband's household. Today, that situation has changed. Now it's a young man who is more likely to live at home and also to move back home if a cohabiting relationship breaks up.

Thus, young men move from the doting care of a mother to the doting care of a girlfriend and then, if things don't work out, they return to the doting care of a mother. In 2000, 7.5 million or 56 percent of men, ages 18 to 24, lived at home, compared to 5.6 million or 43 percent of women in the same age group. The number of men, ages 25 to 34, who live with one or both parents is more than double that of women of the same age, who live in the parental home (2.2 million and 1 million, respectively).[6] According to a recent study of residential patterns among the young, the parental home is more congenial to sons than daughters. Parents are less likely to supervise the social lives of their adult sons or to expect their sons to contribute to housework. Apparently, parents enjoy "doing" for their sons, while they expect daughters to "do" for themselves.[7]

Even men who are able to cook, clean, and maintain a place on their own sometimes relapse as soon as they share a household with a woman. The dependency of males on female nurturance, if it is available, seems to be a persistent pattern. A female teacher I know tells a story that illustrates this point: she divides her sixth grade students into cleanup teams. Each team has certain duties to perform, and the team that sustains the best record for cleaning up wins a prize. In the past, these groups have been same sex. This school year, however, my teacher friend decided to make the teams coed.

Almost at once, the girls began to complain that the boys were not doing their fair share, and upon investigating their complaint, the teacher established that it was legitimate. Once placed in a team with girls, boys who had done a good job cleaning up as members of a same-sex team began to slack off.

When it comes to dividing the work of the household, the boys who grow up to be married men also fail to do their fair share, according to a number of studies. But in recent years, husbands have increased the hours spent on housework and childcare. Though their progress is slow, it is moving in the right direction. Husbands of employed wives have an incentive to contribute to housework and childcare, because they have a shared financial stake in household and children and because they are in a partnership that has a longer time horizon and stronger commitment than cohabitation. Under such circumstances, it makes sense to reach some stable accommodation about the division of family responsibilities. However, because living-together relationships are less secure, both socially and legally, a woman has less leverage to impel the man to change his behavior, short of leaving him.

Some men have an unerring instinct for women who know how to take charge and take care. Competent women who want to find a husband can instead find themselves with a dependent boyfriend on their hands. "It really was like he was a kid," a Midwestern marketing manager says of a former live-in boyfriend. "He was looking to me to tell him what to do and when to do it." "I felt responsible for his success or failure, and he was holding me responsible and it wasn't fair."

Women often believe a cohabiting relationship is inherently more egalitarian than a marriage. In a marriage, some say, they risk falling into traditional gender roles. In a living-together partnership, they are more "role-free." Yet if this notion is sound in theory, it seems to be hard to achieve in practice. In some respects, cohabitation-as-courtship can be as unequal as a traditional 1950s marriage.

CHOOSING COURTSHIP WITHOUT COHABITATION

AT 27, BLAIR HAS ACCOMPLISHED many of the personal and professional goals she set for herself. She finished her baccalaureate in less than four years and took eight months to backpack through Europe and travel the States until she ran out of money. She earned an MBA. She had a series of marketing jobs that led to her current position as an account executive for a Southwestern communications company. She has lived by herself for most of her 20s.

During these years, she had three relationships of about six to eight months each. For a while, she lived in a trendy beach town where the men "didn't get me," she says. "They wanted something 'blonder, taller and more scientifically enlarged.'" When she moved to the city of 700,000 where she now works, she found a more hospitable singles scene. There was less emphasis on money or celebrity looks. She had a lively social life and many dates.

A year or so ago, she attended an economic development conference where she met Jack, the founder and president of a mentoring organization. "When we first met, I thought he came across as too cocky," Blair recalls. "But I guess that's how you have to be if you run your own company at such a young age." Later on, though, she found him the opposite: sweet, smart, and, unlike the intense careerist men she had dated in the past, confident but laid back. "He's all sugar inside," she says.

They began to go out and, at the time that I first interviewed Blair, she had been seeing him exclusively for seven months. She thought he "was the one." The subject of marriage had come up naturally, Blair recalls, as they talked about their future. "We both wanted to have children in our early 30s, and we calculated backwards from then to now. We realized we should be thinking about getting married soon." Another thing that "forced the issue of marriage in a positive way," she says, was that they had not moved in together. "It was such a hassle to live apart that we began to think about marriage," she says.

A few months later, I checked back with Blair. She and Jack had gotten engaged and were planning a spring wedding. Jack picked out a ring in November but kept it a secret until he was able to pay it off. He also left work early one day, flew several hundred miles to her parents' house, and asked their blessing for their marriage. Blair knew they would be getting engaged soon, but she didn't know exactly when it would be official. New Year's and then Valentine's Day passed. The week after Valentine's Day, Jack took her out for dinner at a beachfront restaurant. He asked the waiter to pack up their desserts to go. They took the two boxes out on the beach to eat. One box had a piece of cheesecake. The other had a rose with a ring slipped onto the stem.

The couple plans to move in together right before their wedding. But until then, Blair says that living apart has been a better way to prepare for marriage than living together. It hasn't been easy or convenient to maintain separate places, she says. But she thinks it has helped her make the right decision about marriage. Living together is easy, and that's the problem. If it is easy, she says, it might also be easy to think he was the right guy when he wasn't. Blair and Jack have also started taking a marriage class at a local church. "We're not at all religious," she says, "but the church was the only place we could find such a course. We are really looking forward to the preparation, and it helps to be able to go off in our separate corners and think about what we've read before we talk about it together." Blair likes this time of anticipating and preparing for their life together. They're getting ready for the lifelong changes that come with marriage.

In the pattern of their early life course, Emily and Blair look a lot alike. They both had college education and travel followed by progressively responsible jobs and professional career development. They also had similar romantic biographies: a few relationships of short duration before they meet a man they want to marry. However, at this point, their stories diverge. Both women begin a serious relationship during the critical time when they began to search for a life partner. Emily enters her partnership at 30 with a cohabitation-as-courtship arrangement. Blair begins her relationship at 27 in a courtship without cohabitation arrangement. Emily invested five crucial years in order to find out that her boyfriend wasn't suitable, or interested, in marriage. Blair spent less than a year in order to confirm that her boyfriend was "the one," and that he shared her desire for marriage and children in the near future. By forsaking the conveniences of cohabitation, she was able to avoid getting prematurely enmeshed in a relationship before she knew exactly what she needed to know about Jack's character, conduct, and intentions. Importantly, they talked about marriage as a "natural" progression of their relationship, and they "did the math" together on when they would like to have children. Clearly, Jack was on the same page when it came to their plans for a family.

Blair and Jack's conversations about marriage were part of the deliberate conduct of a serious courtship. By living apart, they were able to talk about their future life together. This might not have seemed so necessary if they were already living together. In fact, living together can inhibit discussion about some of the big issues—children, money, and career—that arise in a marriage. Also, Blair was able to avoid wasting valuable time. If their romance had foundered, or failed, she still had enough time to find a more suitable mate. Even more important, Blair exhibited an unusual mindfulness about her goals, a clarity and seriousness of purpose. It helped that she had already made a firm personal policy decision about cohabitation before she met Jack. Before it ever came up, she already knew her answer to the question: "Should we live together?"

CHAPTER VI

THE SEARCH BEGINS

THE NEW SINGLE WOMAN CAN EASILY reach her mid-20s without having the slightest idea of how to go about finding someone who would be suitable for her to marry. Her college experience of hooking up and hanging out isn't meant to prepare her for selecting a marriage mate. Though she may have had a limited number of sexual encounters and some great guy friends to hang out with, she hasn't had enough opportunities to experience the kind of relationship that would lead to marriage. As one undergraduate at a small Northeastern liberal arts college told a researcher, "I never . . . in a million years picture myself meeting somebody here . . . I don't feel like I've had enough experiences to be able to meet somebody now that I know for sure [I would be able to marry] . . . I feel like I need to have a lot more, I think, encounters before I really find someone."[1]

And if college isn't the right place to find a life mate, the years after college aren't the right time. In her early 20s, the new single woman has other things to accomplish before seeking a husband. A 23-year-old graduate student in engineering tells me that she wouldn't "mind" if someone great came along but she is "busy with other things" and "it's not important to her right now" to find a serious boyfriend. At this stage, she is more interested in a man of the moment rather than a man for all seasons. For now, she would like someone who would "give her a hug," "tell her she's attractive," and "do fun things, like hiking" with her. It is too early to think about a more serious commitment. In an online posting, another young woman says that she is looking for a commitment "along the lines of 'you're cool, I like you, and I don't want to date anyone else.'"

But, beyond her view of the immediate moment, the new single woman doesn't always realize how dramatically the mating world has changed, and how the changes will affect her ability to find a future life mate. And this is not surprising. Changes in the mating system, unlike changes in the weather, aren't forecast on the nightly news. What's more, during the course of her formative education, she has had no help in understanding or preparing for her transition from an early career path to a later marriage track. She has been bereft of useful advice, social support, and plausible models.

In the absence of such knowledge, it is easy for her to assume that the mating system is aligned with her desires and will help to reach whatever romantic goals she sets for herself. However, once she gets into her mid-20s and begins to think more seriously about finding someone to marry, she may discover that this assumption doesn't meet the test of experience. Although she may have learned by then what she doesn't want in a life partner, she hasn't yet found a way to get what she does want.

Meanwhile, her social network, her opportunities, and her sense of time have all changed. When she was in college or just out of college, nearly everyone in her social group was unmarried and only intermittently partnered. Almost no one was looking for a life partner, much less settling down. Now they're partnering up and getting married. When she was in college or just out of college, she had access to a pool of never-married single men who were similarly matched in their age, educational attainment, and socioeconomic background. Now, the pool is more diverse in its composition, more various in its goals, and more geographically spread out. When she was in college or just out of college, she had plenty of time for career first and marriage and children later. Now, she is aware that the amount of time available for her to achieve the goal of marriage-and-children is finite. Accordingly, she must make good use of every month and every year.

At 26 or 27, she can find herself on social, emotional, and geographic terrain that is very different from when she was 21—or even 25. She has reached a critical juncture. She has time to find a loving mate, but not a lot of time to waste on the other kind. It's important to avoid drift and delay. In order to do that, however, she has to have a clear picture of the terrain. That way, she can be mindful of where she stands, where she wants to go, and how to avoid the pitfalls that might stand in her way.

WHERE SHE STANDS

FOR A SENSE OF WHERE THE NEW single woman stands on today's mating landscape, start by considering the figure below. It uses Census data to plot a recent distribution of college-educated women by age and marital status. Their ages run along the bottom of the figure and range from 22 to 41. The percentage of women who are single at each age is shown along the left side, high percentages at the top, low percentages at the bottom.[2]

PERCENTAGE OF COLLEGE-EDUCATED WOMEN WHO ARE SINGLE, BY AGE

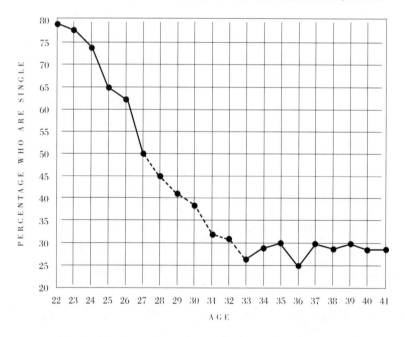

At age 24, slightly more than a quarter (26 percent) are married. Presumably, for nearly all of them, this is a first marriage. Though we can't know for sure, there's a good chance that many of these young women met their future husbands during or shortly after college or graduate school, perhaps through a college-based connection. They could have been students on the same coed campus, or they might have met through college friends. And quite likely, their romance evolved from activities connected to school social life.

Forty years ago, the married percentage for 24-year-old college women was twice as high, at 53 percent. For 25 year olds, it jumped to 72 percent.[3] Still, the current proportion is hardly negligible. Though the old system of romantic courtship is only a faded remnant, the college-based mating pool still offers women the convenience of a geographically concentrated and prequalified group of peer men. And the college women who are willing to follow the old timetable for marriage can avail themselves of this pool.

Clearly, though, a rising percentage of college women haven't been interested in using the advantages of the campus mating pool during their undergraduate years. At age 24, as the figure indicates, almost three-quarters of college women are single. From ages 24 to 34, the percentage of those who are single declines and then levels off. If you look at the lower right corner of the figure, you see that the percentage of women who are single holds fairly steady at roughly 28 percent. But the steadiness of the pattern is deceptive. It seems to imply stability. But the circumstances behind it are dynamic.

We know that some of the women of these ages, 35 to 41 and beyond, had married and are now getting divorced. This would make the percentage of women who are single go up. But it doesn't actually go up. It varies a bit, but essentially holds steady, at 28 percent. What this implies is clear: just as some women are entering the single ranks via divorce, a roughly equal number of other women are leaving those ranks via marriage. At these ages, consequently, first marriages are still occurring. Indeed, of the 28 percent of the women who are single, only about half are those who at this point have never married.

Moreover, not all of the women who are single stand at the same spot on the mating landscape. Their location depends on their age, their goals, and their access to a pool of prospective mates. There are at least two characteristic types: the straddler and the searcher.

THE STRADDLER

ROUGHLY SPEAKING, THE STRADDLER can be as young as 22 or as old as 27. She is a straddler because it is easy for her to have one foot in the early marriage system and one in the relationships system, and to move back and forth between the two. She is still close enough in time to her college network of friends to find prospective mates through those ties. At the same time, as she moves from the campus to the city, she has also gained access to a large group of new men. In this location on the landscape, she has good mating prospects. So good, as a matter of fact, that she can take a carefree approach. She doesn't have to be conscious of her location, concerned about her timetable, or fixated on her long-term goals. Moreover, since she is in the prime years of her youth, she is able to attract lots of men. Her mating goals are fluid and open-ended. For her, the game is to have fun, try out a variety of partnerships, and put off any serious commitments until some later date. Though she may see marriage as an eventual goal, it can seem as far away as her first social security check. In fact, she may be looking for a relationship that expressly is not designed to lead to marriage. As one such woman explained in a posting in the *Washington Post*: "I'm not looking to get married. I'm only 22! I just want someone to hang out with, to kiss me goodnight, and maybe wake up next to me in the morning."[4] Another woman in her early 20s likened the kind of relationship she was looking for to "a sleepover with my best friend." If seeking a future life mate is not a pressing concern, neither is time. The straddler enjoys the luxury of a long time horizon. And in her first years after college she may not yet be so high up the career ladder that she has to spend all her time at work. She probably has the leisure and the energy to party, go to clubs and Happy Hours, and hang out with friends on the weekend or after work.

She can find peer single men who are available for sleepovers or hanging out or coed friendship. It isn't hard to find loveless sex or sexless love or even love and sex for the short term. "It doesn't make sense to rely on one person to meet all your needs," a 28-year-old woman once remarked to me. "Our generation diversifies. We might have one person for sex, one to go out club-hopping, another to share thoughts and feelings." Indeed, such low-commitment mating goals are in synch with those of many of her male peers: men are similarly focused on avoiding any permanent romantic attachments until they gain independence, life experience, and financial stability. For these 20 somethings, comradeship has replaced courtship. Or, to borrow a political metaphor, the aspiration to union has been abandoned for the more modest goal of confederacy.

THE SHIFT

AT 28 OR SO, AND FOR THE FIRST time in her life, the single woman finds herself in the unmarried minority. (The proportion of college-educated 28-year-olds who are single is 45 percent.) She's now at a different location on the mating landscape. At this age, she might have reached the end of the school and work path set forth by the Girl Project. She's earned her baccalaureate, and perhaps a graduate degree or two, crisscrossed the globe, served her community, gained traction in her career, and achieved economic independence. She's enjoyed a decade or more of liberated sexuality, had a relationship or two that didn't work out, and developed a strong sense of what she is seeking in a mate. She might now be ready to turn to the pursuit of a recent, or deferred, goal: marriage and children.

If so, however, she is now more removed in time from the college mating pool. Her school ties may have worn thin, or, if they remain strong, they may not generate as many available single men as they once did. Some of those guys from her college days have married. If only for mating purposes, she has "aged out" out of the college network. It is harder and harder for her to draw upon its resources or exploit its advantages. She is ceasing to be a straddler.

Moreover, she is no longer as young as she once was. A fresh crop of younger women may also have arrived on the scene. For these reasons, and because she is now focused on marriage as her mating goal, she faces a greater challenge than does a young woman who is still interested in a relationship without a ring. Thus, at the very time when she begins to feel ready for marriage, she is shifting from a location where she could take advantage of both her college network and the relationships pool to a place where she is now marginal to both. This is what Christina, whom we met in the first chapter, experienced as she turned 30. It's at this point that such a woman might wonder if there are any good men left.

My Best Friend's Wedding offers a portrait of a single woman who is going through this shift. Successful New York restaurant critic and author Juliane Potter (Julia Roberts) has always disdained tradition-al feminine priorities like love and marriage. She hates weddings and never attends. Although she's had lots of relationships during her 20s, she's loved only one man, her "best friend" Michael O'Neal. Michael was her boyfriend for a "hot" month during their under-graduate years at Brown, but since then, they've been through every-thing together: losing jobs, losing parents, losing lovers. They've been soul mates for nine years. In fact, they've made a Plan B agree-ment that if neither one is married by age 28, they'll marry each other. But Juliane has been so busy with her recent book tour that she's not even had time to talk to Michael for a while. It's only after she gets an urgent voice mail message from him that she is reminded of her fast-approaching 28th birthday and their agreement.

When she reaches Michael, as fans of the movie know, she doesn't get the news she expected. He's calling to announce his wed-ding on the coming weekend. His bride-to-be, Kimmy (Cameron Diaz), is 20, beautiful, smart, and rich. She's "all wrong" for me, says Michael, but he can't help himself. He's never felt this way about anyone before. Juliane is shocked, upset, and jealous. It's not that Michael has betrayed her in any way. Their relationship has been about being free to do what you wanted to do. It's just that she always expected that he would be available if she wanted to go to their Plan B, the get-married-to-each-other option. Now she's likely to lose that option. More than that, she's always counted on having first place in his affections. Now she has a serious rival.

Juliane resorts to all kinds of underhanded stratagems and dirty tricks to get Michael to call off the wedding. But nothing works. She only succeeds in getting Michael and Kim to realize how much they love each other. The wedding goes off as planned, with Juliane as the maid of honor. At the reception, she's left all alone, until her gay "best friend" George arrives and pulls her out of her funk and onto the dance floor: "Maybe there won't be marriage, maybe there won't be sex, but, by God," he assures her, "there will be dancing."

It has been a tradition in Hollywood films for the single career woman to come to a crossroads where she is forced to decide between work and love. According to this cinematic formula, she isn't allowed to have both. In *Broadcast News*, for example, Jane Craig, the Type A television producer played by Holly Hunter, must give up love for the sake of her work. In the final scene, when she reunites with the two men she might have married, she has to face the consequences of her choice. They're married and content, while she's had to give up that dream. She's dating someone, but the film leaves you with the feeling that Jane will always be lonely and alone.

My Best Friend's Wedding breaks with this convention. It doesn't force the classic choice between career and marriage. It's the story of two smart, attractive, ambitious women who look a lot alike on paper but are at different locations on the mating landscape. Kim is 20 and a junior in college when she meets Michael. She didn't plan to fall in love and get married; in fact, she tells Juliane, "I used to be just like you." But she's made a decision to marry the man she loves and to postpone her career plans in order to spend time with him. For the moment, she is a marriage girl in a semblance of the earlier marriage system.

Juliane's situation is different. She's nearly eight years older than Kim, she's put love on hold while she gets ahead in her career, and she's barely thought about finding a soul mate. She's been hold-ing an option to marry a member of her college network, but now she has lost it. She'd always thought that she could marry when she was ready, but now she realizes that she can't just order up marriage when she wants.

The movie leaves each woman with the inevitable consequences of the path she takes. Kim marries Michael, a "good man" who loves her. But she still has to come to terms with her deferred career ambitions. Indeed, her marriage leaves some big problems unresolved: will she put her own career on hold forever? Will Michael trade the low-paying job he loves for a high-prestige job he hates in his father-in-law's enterprise? At the end of the movie, you can't help but wonder about Michael's observation that Kim is "all wrong" for him. What if it proves to be correct?

Juliane is hardly doomed to a lonely singlehood. No matter what happens in her future love life, she's still got her gay best friend; George isn't going to leave her for a younger woman. With him, "there will always be dancing." And she hasn't really lost Michael, either. He'll probably call her when he gets back from his honeymoon. Nevertheless, with Michael's wedding to Kim, Juliane has lost the chance to be chosen by the only man she's ever loved. If Juliane wants to find someone to marry, it may not be easy to find another man like the man she first met in college.

THE SEARCHERS

AFTER 28, THE NEW SINGLE WOMAN is solidly situated in the relationships system. In this new location, she might have one of at least two mating goals. One is to continue to seek a relationship, or to remain in an existing relationship. If so, then her mating goal is well aligned with what the relationships system can offer. In her late 20s or early 30s, such a woman can probably find men who are interested in having casual sex, short-term relationships, or a living-together union. She might be called a "relationships girl" in the relationships system.

The characters in *Sex and the City* fit this profile. By the end of its fourth season, all four had settled into the relationships system, perhaps for the long haul. Charlotte, the most traditional of the four, ended her brief marriage and became a dating single again. Carrie turned down a marriage proposal from her boyfriend, Aidan, and lost Mr. Big to the West Coast. Miranda got pregnant and had a child with her ex-boyfriend, but marriage to him, or anyone else, wasn't in the picture. And, after suspecting for a few episodes that she might have fallen into nothing less than monogamous love, Samantha resumed her sexual prowl.

Another mating goal is marriage-and-a-child. The marriage-minded woman has deferred this goal until she is older, and she has gained some of the advantages of waiting longer to contemplate it. She may be more mature, financially stable, and have had more life experience than a similarly educated woman who marries in her early to mid-20s. Indeed, as some scholars theorize, such a woman may be better able to make a wise choice of a partner at this age, be more likely to have a marriage that lasts, and be more competent as a parent. Nevertheless, a marriage-minded woman in this location faces a challenge. It's not insurmountable, but it does require a high level of mindfulness about the way she spends her time and the choices she makes.

To fulfill her desire for marriage, she will probably have to make a conscious effort to find a suitable mate. This will make her a searcher. The searcher is defined by her age, her mating agenda, and her sense of time limits: she is in her late 20s or older, her goal is marriage-and-children, and she wants to achieve her goals sooner rather than later.

However, her mating goal and her location on the mating landscape are not perfectly aligned. She isn't a marriage-minded woman in the campus-based marriage system, the way her mother might have been, and she isn't a relationships-oriented woman in the relationships system, the way a Carrie Bradshaw might be. She's a marriage-minded woman in a relationships system. This is like being an Amish woman at a rave. Her mating goals make her different from others in the crowd.

Since she has a more ambitious goal than other women in the relationships system, it might well take her a longer time to reach it. First of all, she has to find an available man whom she adores and who adores her back. Then she has to be confident that this adorable man shares her aspirations for having and rearing children together. What's more, he has to be ready and willing to do so in a marriage partnership.

However, as she looks for a man to become her husband and the father of her children, she must do it in a mating pool that includes men whose goals are at odds with hers. Not all men are interested in marriage and children. Some men will want little more than sex, others will want a living-together relationship with a commitment (at least on her side) to monogamy, and still others will want to live together for an indefinite period of time and "see what happens." Some won't be sure what they want. And others will be recovering from a traumatic divorce or breakup and will want to have someone to boost their bruised egos, minister to them sexually, and, if they have children, help them with the kids. For a searcher, consequently, a crucial task in the search is to screen and sort men. She must eliminate the guys whose agendas don't match hers. And she must do it quickly.

In addition, a searcher is likely to discover that she isn't the only Girl Project graduate who's in the mating market. There are other searchers like her—late 20s and older, accomplished, well-employed, and looking for a husband. Then, there are women who are like her, but who are interested in levels of commitment below marriage. This gives them the advantage of having a larger pool of prospective mates, since some available single men will prefer a lower-commitment relationship to a marriage. Also, there are women who are just as well educated and professionally accomplished as the searcher, but are several years younger and are also seeking marriage-and-children.

Finally, two other categories of women are in the same market: women who are her age or younger, just as well educated, but not as dedicated to career; and women who are her age or younger but aren't as well educated. The searcher is often surprised to find herself in the market with women in the last two categories. Although she has had little guidance about love and marriage (as opposed to the management of her sexuality) during her formative years, she has learned a great deal about her considerable worth as a person of great accomplishment, vivid spirit, and bold initiative—the very embodiment of girl power. The domains of school and work have distinguished her from the women who went to safety schools and got degrees in early childhood education. But this doesn't mean that men, for mating purposes, draw the same distinction. As she might discover, her favorable status in the domain of work doesn't necessarily translate into an equally favorable status in the domain of love.

The fact is, not all career-primary professional men—the searcher's peers in education and achievement—want to marry women who have equally ambitious career plans. This doesn't mean that today's young single men don't want their future wives to work. On the contrary. According to studies conducted by the National Marriage Project, young men expect their future wives to work for pay outside the home, to contribute to the family income, and to have their own career plans and interests even if they spend some time out of the work force caring for small children. However, some career-primary men would prefer wives who are well educated, successfully employed, but not as ambitious in their careers as the men themselves. For these men, life is easier and their own career path smoother if they can find a wife who is content with a less demanding job or a slower pace of career advancement. Thus, all else being equal, a cardiac surgeon might prefer to marry a biochemist who works flex-time for a pharmaceutical company rather than another cardiac surgeon.

In addition to the challenge of identifying a suitable man whose goals are for marriage and children, the searcher has to be conscious of time. She can't invest time in a relationship that isn't going to lead to marriage. This isn't a reason to panic or to feel tyrannized by the biological clock. On the contrary, if a marriage-minded woman knows how to protect and conserve her time, she can feel a greater sense of control and confidence in her search. Fortunately, if the searcher can learn to identify the time traps in her search, she will also be able to identify the men who are not likely to share her ambitions for marriage.

At its current stage of development, however, the relationships system offers the searcher few of the social supports and resources that used to be available to single women in the marriage system. It doesn't give her a good information and referral network. To be sure, she has friends and colleagues who can fix her up with men but, as she gets older, this network gets weaker. Its members move away or move on. And when she turns to some of the social institutions that often have served as a source of pre-qualified prospects, such as faith communities, she finds that these sources might not be very helpful to her. In many denominations, there is a bias toward serving married couples and their children. Single young adults are often overlooked as members of the faith community and neglected as singles seeking marriage partners. In short, there is no contemporary courtship system to fit the new single woman's timetable or goals.

As a consequence, the searcher must take the initiative to look on her own. She has to do her own qualifying and screening of prospective mates. Moreover, she must do it by drawing on a pool of single men who are diverse in their agendas, often difficult to read, and geographically dispersed. She must gather information on her own rather than through knowledgeable third parties. She must seek sources of expertise and advice from those who are outside of her own immediate circle of family and friends and colleagues. At the same time, she must see herself in a hopeful light: not as a romantically desperate singleton, but as a woman whose successful search might be featured in the "Vows" column of the *New York Times*.

"VOWS" GIRLS IN A RELATIONSHIPS WORLD

NO ONE HAS DRAWN A MORE romantically hopeful portrait of the searcher than Lois Smith Brady, "Vows" columnist for the Sunday *Times* and the author of a book of real-life love stories, *Love Lessons*. For more than a decade, she has reported on the weddings of high-status couples. With imagination and insight, she transformed the staid wedding notice, with its starchy recital of nuptial facts, into something far more compelling and dramatic. Indeed, "Vows" is not really about marriage or weddings at all. It is about the search for love. In her pages, the search is a long and arduous one—but, ultimately, it is successful.

Though "Vows" features brides as old as 80, most of the "Vows" girls fit the model of the searcher: they are older than the average bride, intelligent, spirited, iconoclastic, focused, and full of opinions, wit, and energy. For the most part, they have elite credentials and important careers, though some are free spirits, artists, or adventurers. No matter what they do, however, "Vows" girls share common characteristics. They are fiercely independent and strong-minded: indeed, even as they marry, they worry about surrendering to the institution of marriage and its retro conventions. When Megan Mulry, 29, married Jeffrey Huisinga, 33, she made him agree not to call her his "wife."[5] Shasta Jensen, 30, was more a relationships girl than a "Vows" girl until she found personal trainer Greg Waggoner, 29, who "gives me my space and freedom . . . and just never brings me down."[6]

Yet though many of these women have done a brilliant job of finding themselves, they've had a hard time finding love. Some have been too busy with their careers to search for a mate, while others have suffered bad breakups, divorce, loneliness, or the death of a spouse. Some have had a string of dating disasters, like Wendy Zuckerwise, 45, who had managed the Donna Karan department at Bergorf Goodman for 15 years but had trouble managing her love life. For her, "horrible dates and broken hearts were as common as snowstorms in Colorado. Each year she experienced several."[7] Others are grieving, like Susan Fragnoli, 39, fresh from a divorce, whose daily struggle was not to break down and cry in front of her boss and her kids.[8] Or like diehard Brooklynite Heidi Smith, 37, who moved back to New York from San Francisco when her mother developed cancer. After her mother died, Heidi found herself sad, alone, unemployed, and unsure about what to do next in her life. "I would go to the MAC counters at the make-up store and say, "I have no foundation in my life, but I'll take some foundation on my face.""[9]

But just when "Vows" girls least expect it, they find love—at an art gallery, a concert, a bookstore, on the uptown B train, or a pediatric clinic in Katmandu. But once found, love does not always lead smoothly or directly to marriage. There are snags and setbacks, fears and vicissitudes, to overcome along the way. "Vows" couples have to face tests and trials. They have to endure the torment of waiting for a divorce to become final before they can marry again. Or they live great distances apart and have to schedule time to be together. They are frightened of making the same mistakes that caused them heartbreak in the past. Sometimes, they lose their nerve and call off the wedding. In one case, for example, the "Vows" couple cancels their wedding at the last moment but carries on with the reception and trip to Mexico. (They marry later in a private civil ceremony on a beach in Mexico.)[10]

By shifting the focus from the marriage ceremony to a story of the successful search, Brady not only transformed the traditional wedding notice but also vastly expanded the reading audience for "Vows." Her stories are not designed for the social register crowd or for smug marrieds. They are for single women who identify with the story of the long search for the right man. In "Vows," they find stories of women who resemble them: smart, sophisticated, and stalled in their search for lasting love. To these readers, the long and winding road to marriage looks familiar.

Brady is ideal as a chronicler of love and marriage in the relationships system, because she believes that love can happen at any age. Indeed, she says, as you get older in chronological years, you get younger in love. As one of the men in *Love Lessons* tells her: It's like the Bob Dylan lyric: "I was so much older then. I'm younger than that now."[11] What's more, according to Brady, love has its own logic and its own sense of time. There is nothing a woman can do to hurry love or to make it happen. "Whenever anyone asks me about love . . . I always say wait for that feeling, wait, wait, wait. Wait with the patience of a Buddhist fly fisherman."[12]

"Vows" is admirably faithful to a romantic conception of the mating search in the relationships system, but not to its sociological realities. Indeed, much of its portrait of the search runs contrary to evidence and experience. Searching for a mate doesn't get easier as women get older. It gets harder. As the Princeton projections suggest, its difficulty doesn't rise with age as much as it did in the past. But it rises nevertheless. For another, the notion that love will find you is not reliable. It can happen, of course. But a marriage-minded woman in the relationships world wouldn't be wise to count on it. And the Buddhist fly fisherman approach isn't recommended for the woman in her 30s who wants to have children. Generally, searchers cannot afford to take what one man profiled in Brady's book called "the slow train to We."[13] They must find ways to conserve and manage their time. The new single woman who is looking for a husband in the relationships system can't allow men to set the pace and timing of her search. If she does, she is limiting her opportunity to reach her goal of marriage sooner rather than later. To the best of her considerable abilities, the searcher must take charge of her own search.

CHAPTER VII

WORKING AT LOVE

IN HER SELF-MANAGED SEARCH FOR LOVE, the new single woman is turning to the tools and technologies of work. The habits and disciplines of the workplace are well suited to the nature of her search. They aim at time and market efficiencies, and her timetable and mating market call for such efficiencies. Indeed, three popular and well-known approaches to the mating search all share one feature in common. They help the searcher make the most of a scarce and valuable resource: namely, her time.

THE RULES

THE RULES POSES AS A CHATTY, girly volume on relationships, but it is really a tough-minded business book. Like a number of such books, it is based on a time-management philosophy. Its core principle is that marriage-minded women have to treat time the way Victorian women treated sex: they can't give it away promiscuously or casually. They have to use it as a source of power and advantage.

In 1995, *The Rules* came out of nowhere and became a surprise bestseller. Written by Ellen Fein and Sherrie Schneider, two then-married women (Fein later divorced), the book claimed to offer an effective and time-honored way to get a husband. Women raced to buy it. It sold 2 million copies and was translated into 27 languages. Its spectacular popularity inspired two successor books, *The Rules II* (1997) and *The Rules for Marriage* (2001), as well as websites, seminars, and book clubs. "It's not just a book, but a movement," a reviewer for *Time* reported.

Almost as soon as it appeared, however, *The Rules* provoked sneers and criticism. Many women objected to its ruthlessly rigid principles. (Rule # 7: Don't Accept a Saturday Night Date after Wednesday; Rule # 11: Always End the Date First; Rule # 14: No More Than Casual Kissing on the First Date.) They seemed manipulative, artificial, and anti-feminist: "trite," "stupid," "appalling," and "a throwback" were a few of the adjectives tossed at them. Some of the severest critics were men. Bill Maher ridiculed the book and his guests, the two authors, on *Politically Incorrect*, his then late night show. Other men scoffed at the book's argument that women should play hard to get, insisting that men responded to friendly

women who didn't play games. Still other enterprising men published parodies of *The Rules*, written from the guy perspective. Titles
included: *The Rules for Getting Laid; The Code: Getting What You
Want from Women without Marrying Them!;* and *The Guide: The
Essential Resource for Picking up Girls.*

But the controversy simply brought *The Rules* to the attention of
more women, and many read it—though some did so surreptitiously.
Its appeal was impossible to ignore, or to wave off as mere backlash.
Too many smart women were intrigued by its promise of success in
finding a husband. One woman spoke for many when she wrote in an
online review: "As a woman who loves to quote Gloria Steinem and
Naomi Wolf, it's not easy to admit [reading *The Rules*] but I'm also a
romantic and would like to marry before I'm 40."

The Rules claimed that its advice was time-tested, something
that women's grandmothers had known but that today's women had
forgotten. Yet, despite its nod to ancestral wisdom, it is an utterly
contemporary book, a perfect reflection of its time. *The Rules* is
implicitly in tune with the conditions that give rise to the new single
woman and her search.

For one thing, *The Rules* was one of the first books to demon-
strate that the educated single woman was a prime new audience for
dating advice. Traditionally, books on courtship and dating were
written for the teen and college set; their Q & As focused on issues
ranging from curfews to corsages. With the rise of the new single
woman, however, a new market for dating opened up. However, these
women were older, independent, experienced, and not dependent on
marriage, or men, for an identity or a life. As *The Rules* puts it: "You
are a very fulfilled person—stable, functional, and happy—with a
career, friends, and hobbies . . . and you are perfectly capable of liv-

ing with or without him. You are not an empty vessel waiting for him to fill you up, support you, or give you a life."[1] Nor were such women inexperienced in love; in fact, if *The Rules*' portrait of them was accurate, their problem was just the opposite. They were sophisticated women who had had too much experience. They were suffering from the symptoms of relationship fatigue: dumpings, jealousies, rebounds, emotional bruises, and loneliness.

At the same time, like Lois Smith Brady, the authors of *The Rules* recognized that this sophisticated group of older women still wanted to be married. Without apology, therefore, *The Rules* ushers marriage out of the closet. Aren't you tired of the pain and loneliness?, the authors ask. Don't you want real lasting marriage instead of "loveless mergers?"[2] What's more, the authors make it clear that they see no contradiction between one's status as a professional independent woman and one's desire to be married. "We didn't want to give up our liberation," they note, "but neither did we want to come home to empty apartments."[3]

The Rules imparts one crucial insight to its readers: women can be successful in their mating search, but they have to understand that their most valuable resource is their time—both the hours in the day and the years in their life. Moreover, it notes, time is double-edged. It can be a source of vulnerability for a marriage-minded woman, but it can also be the source of her power. It depends on how she uses it. If she squanders her time in a going-nowhere relationship or by living together with a boyfriend without knowing where marriage fits in the picture, she is losing valuable time that she can't get back. At the same time, she is in charge of her own time and how she invests it. So she can use her time to her advantage. And who better to appreciate this insight than a professional woman who knows how valuable her time is in the marketplace and wouldn't dream of wasting it or giving it away without some kind of compensation in return?

This insight provides the basis for the Rules girl's strategy. Her goal is to conserve her time while letting him invest his. By prompting a boyfriend to take the initiative, she gets a better sense of his level of interest. This doesn't guarantee that the relationship will work out, but it offers some objective evidence that he is interested enough in a relationship to actively seek her out and to make a plan to spend his time with her. It protects her from getting prematurely enmeshed in subsidizing his health and happiness—doing his laundry or his tax returns—without any sign of reciprocal commitment of time and attention on his part. Thus, just as earlier generations of women had been counseled to withhold their sexual favors from a suitor in order to get a marriage proposal, so today's *Rules* girls have to learn to hold back on their time until they have some clear expression of romantic interest from a boyfriend.

The Rules' strict legalisms excite controversy and criticism because they seem to take all the spontaneity out of romance. And this criticism is well taken. The rules are robotic and simplistic. Yet their larger purpose is not simple-minded. They are a time management discipline designed to give searchers the same sense of control over the pace and timing of the search as they get over their work schedule with their Daytimers and Palm Pilots. The target reader for *The Rules* is a woman who has been trained to set goals, keep lists, and track her billable hours. Time management is something she does well. *The Rules* simply takes a familiar skill, cultivated and prized in work, and applies it to the search for love.

THE INTERNET

IF *THE RULES* GIVES WOMEN A self-help method of managing their time, the Internet provides a new self-directed approach for managing the mating market. Every so often, a new technology emerges at roughly the same time that a new social, cultural, or economic trend takes hold. Together, the technology and the trend then engage in a dense and close interplay. Atomic weapons emerged just as the Cold War began. The birth control pill came into widespread use as the women's movement was getting underway. Television appeared as the postwar consumer economy fell into place. Something similar has happened with mating. The technology of the search engine on the World Wide Web came along just as millions of singles, mostly working adults over the age of 25, were looking for new, more effective ways to conduct a successful mating search. It is likely to be as influential in shaping the patterns of mating in the early 21st century as the internal combustion engine was in shaping the patterns of youthful dating in the early 20th century.

Online dating is less than ten years old, but its growth has been phenomenal. In 1995, online dating sites barely existed. Today, there are more than 2,500 such websites.[4] The large sites, such as Match.com and Yahoo Personals, have close to 4 million visitors each month. And this is one of the few online services that people are willing to pay for. Indeed, the large dating websites are among the few financial success stories in the world of e-commerce. Match.com, the largest site, with 3.8 million monthly visitors and more than 382,000 paying subscribers, took in $17.6 million and had $7.6 million in earnings in the fourth quarter of 2001.[5] In addition to the mass sites, there are hundreds of niche sites, such as

AsianFriendFinder.com; ThirdAge.com, an over-45 site; singles with scruples.com; Gayll.com; generous.net, a "fat-pride" site; and so on. Both the mass and niche sites provide access to a larger population of singles than would likely be found in a single geographic location, while also providing ways to sort by characteristics such as gender, age ranges, geographic location, religion, and sexual orientation.

Online dating services offer a fascinating example of the way that a new technology can revive and popularize something that is very old. Advertising for marriage partners—usually brides—is a very traditional mating practice, popular among religious and ethnic groups who follow the custom of arranged marriages, and also once popular in American frontier and immigrant communities, where single men vastly outnumbered single women and where few established social institutions existed to bring rough-edged single men in contact with women who might consider marrying them. Finding brides through the mail was a cheap, efficient, streamlined method for men to widen their search for a wife beyond their immediate geographic area. No wooing was required.

Later, as the nation became more settled, the "mail-order bride" business lost popularity and respectability. It continued to exist but mainly on the seedy margins of the society, a practice favored by men who were seeking young, submissive, uneducated brides from poor countries or who were looking for prostitutes.[6] But the Internet resurrected the personal ad as a respectable method of searching for a prospective spouse. Indeed, in a remarkably short period of time, online searching has become a popular way to seek a romantic partner for a variety of purposes, including but not limited to, marriage.

More to the point, the online search offers access and opportunities to participate in a much wider mating market than that found in a single geographic location. The earlier campus-based mating market placed a lot of peer single men and women within a small geographic area, provided some common meeting places and occasions, and made it easy and convenient for them to get together and socialize during their out-of-class hours. Even places where students did their work—such as the library—often did double duty as a place to go on a "study date."

The Internet does much the same thing for working singles. It pulls together a mating pool made up of people who can be sorted by age, interest, and background. It provides an address in cyberspace where they can meet. And it makes it convenient for them to get together during their available free hours. Online searchers—like campus couples on a study date—can "go out" while they are working. Whenever they have a free moment at work, they can log on to their favorite sites, send a message to someone they met recently, engage in a "chat," or post a personal. And, as many have noted, the practice of online searching overcomes the hurdles of hectic schedules and impossible commutes. Searchers don't have to get into a car or subway to meet someone; they don't have to worry about what they're wearing or how they look when they enter a room in cyberspace; they can go online any time of day or night.

The Internet also offers a time-saving way to replicate a feature of the earlier courtship system: it can create a mating market for elites. Ever since the privileged young have had the freedom to choose their own marriage partners, their privileged families have sought to create an exclusive system of dating and mating for them. In the 18th century, the English upper classes created both a local and national mating market for their offspring. In later centuries, social elites in America established an institutional infrastructure of country day schools, clubs, parties, debutante balls, girls finishing schools, and boys academies or, in the 20th century, collegiate matchups between the Ivy League and Seven Sisters to promote social register marriages. Today, privileged singles are still seeking similarly matched partners, but now it is elite education—and extraordinary feats of educational attainment—rather than social class that make up the basis of elite mating markets. Such markets are created to quite literally bring about brilliant alliances—and, later, brilliant children.

Consider, as two leading examples, the Right Stuff, "the Ivy League of Dating," and Good Genes, Inc., an "exclusive introduction service." These sites resemble the admissions offices at Harvard and Princeton. They select only the best and brightest. Members must be graduates or faculty of Ivy League schools or the other highly selective colleges and universities in the nation.[7] Both sites require proof of educational attainment, such as a transcript, piece of alumni mail, or copy of a graduate degree, as a requirement for membership, and they claim to verify members' credentials. The Right Stuff boasts more than 4,000 members in the United States, Canada, and Europe and carries the slogan: "Smart is sexy."

These sites are places where the searcher can meet the kind of men she might have met back in the classroom or the quadrangle— if she hadn't been so busy working on her second degree. Now the Internet gives her access to an elite cybercampus where she can conduct her search. In the postings on these sites, virtually all the female searchers are educational hyperachievers. Not only do they have the requisite elite educational credentials, but some boast double Ivy League degrees or triple degrees from other elite schools. A representative posting from a 37-year-old Californian: UCLA JD (nearly done); Stanford double PhDs. Another, from a Massachusetts "health care attorney," reads: Stanford AB '87, JD '99, Berkeley MPH '93. Yet another from a SBW (single black woman), Brown '82, Wesleyan '88, UPenn Law '91. And then there are the postings from women with eclectic backgrounds, like the "internist with a degree in philosophy" or "model in Paris for ten years, followed by a BA in CompLit from Columbia." What's more, judging from some ads, these women never stop acquiring academic credentials. A 38-year-old lawyer: "I received a bachelor's degree in International Studies from Johns Hopkins and a law degree from Harvard. I received a master's degree in politics from Princeton and am a doctoral student at Princeton now." Or the following:

My undergraduate years were spent at the Manhattan School of Music, during which I also performed as a violinist with a number of orchestras in the city. Then I went on for an MA at Columbia, also in Music. However, about four years ago, I received an MBA and started a career in banking. Currently I am with J.P. Morgan Chase as a Policy Analyst. In my spare time, I still perform and am working on a PhD part-time.

This online sample of ads probably includes a mixture of the marriage-minded and the relationships-oriented. Given the euphemisms for marriage, and the obvious turn-off of seeming desperate for marriage, it's hard to tell for sure who is searching for a marriage partner and who is not. Nonetheless, many women use language highly suggestive of marriage: "I'm looking for an independent, thoughtful, eclectic, loving man (29 to 42) for the whole shebang," writes one ad placer.

SPEEDDATING

ONLINE DATING IS JUST THE FIRST step in identifying someone who might be suitable for a romantic relationship. There has to be
a next step, which is a face-to-face meeting. This sometimes takes a
while to arrange, especially if the couple lives far apart. And oftentimes, when people finally do meet, they are disappointed, or have been
misled, by their date's physical appearance. (Photos exchanged on the
Internet notoriously fudge on a person's age, hair, weight, and height.)

This is not a problem with SpeedDating, a low-tech, offline system that helps people arrive at a quick "yes," "no," or "maybe" decision based on a face-to-face encounter. SpeedDating, a nonprofit
introduction service, is for Jewish singles, but its innovative approach
to meeting and matching has now spawned non-Jewish imitations,
including the for-profit 8Minute Dating, Nanodate, InstadateNY,
10Minute Match, Brief Encounters, and Gay Sprint Dating.[8]

Like the other time-conserving approaches to the search,
SpeedDating organizes and rationalizes the matchmaking process.
As many singles have heard, SpeedDating resembles a version of
musical chairs. Men and women sit across from each other and talk
for seven minutes; a bell sounds and they move to the next person
for the next seven minutes in the rotation. At the end of the session,
everyone fills out a scorecard, indicating their level of interest in the
people they've met and turns it in to the SpeedDating organizers who
contact only those singles whose cards indicate mutual interest.

For the female searcher, the chief attraction of SpeedDating (or
its non-Jewish imitations) is its time-saving feature. It is an efficient
way to meet a lot of people in a short time. No one has to suffer
through a four-hour, doomed-from-the-first-five-minutes date. A

woman knows quickly whether or not she feels what the French call "le click." In addition to saving time on the first meeting, SpeedDating also prevents wasting time and emotion over rejection. Because the encounter lasts only seven minutes, a female searcher can't feel terribly hurt if she is not picked by someone she is attracted to. As in job interviewing, so in the SpeedDating interview: it is easier to be passed over after a first interview than it is to be rejected after you are called back for a second and third interview.

EACH OF THESE TIME-SAVING approaches fits the searcher's repertoire of skills and aptitudes. She knows how to use the tools and technologies of work. She has skills as a time manager, multi-tasker, problem solver, goal setter, and project leader. What's more, as a woman who is accustomed to taking initiative, she can chart her own course. She doesn't have to be subject to the vagaries and uncertainties of chance encounters, exchanges of business cards with strangers at a bar or club, or quick assessments based on weight or looks. She doesn't have to wait passively for love to find her. She can create her own opportunities and maximize her chances for success. Indeed, if a smart woman can't count on a courtship system that fits her purposes and timetable, she can turn to the habits of mind and disciplines of the workplace that have served her so well.

WHEN LOVE BECOMES A THIRD SHIFT

STILL, THERE IS SOMETHING POIGNANT, even troubling, about the metamorphosis of love into a new kind of female work. Consider the case of Lesley Friedman, a lawyer and successful entrepreneur. Her search for a mate was profiled in a 1998 *Wall Street Journal* article by Robert McGough, "If You Can't Get a Man with a Gun, Big Bucks Might Work."[9] A graduate of Mount Holyoke College and NYU Law School, Ms. Friedman has made so much money—$21 million to be exact—that she is able to retire after eight stressful years of work. Then she turns to a neglected area of her life and decides to make a second career out of finding a husband. She gives herself five years to reach the goal.

To reach her goal, she takes a businesslike approach. She assembles a staff of consultants, including an image consultant to help her work on herself. She wangles invitations to tony charity and political fund raisers. She buys a share in a house in East Hampton so she can go to parties there. She spends lavishly, on a new sexier wardrobe, haircut, cosmetic dentistry, contributions to the fund-raising efforts, and consultant services. What's more, she uses her negotiating skills when a promising prospect asks for sex after a second date. She tells the gentleman friend that she will sleep with him if he will promise her "12 weeks of monogamy" in return. Her fallback position: she's willing to settle for six weeks. However, he doesn't agree to the deal, and their relationship fizzles.

Undeterred, she resorts to other business tactics: she networks at fund raisers and creates a stir by telling a Democratic fund raiser that she will give the party $100,000 if he introduces her to a man she marries, a gambit she calls "incentivizing her sales force." She treats another dating disaster as if it were a "sales call." She asks the man for feedback on what he didn't like about her (she's too focused on finding a mate, he says) and then tries to convince him of her positive qualities, as if she were a product in the development stage. But none of her business strategies get her closer to her goal. At the story's conclusion, Friedman is still determined. She is going to work harder to "prequalify" her candidates just as she once prequalified her clients.

Extreme? Of course. But this is what makes the story so revealing. It offers a dystopic vision of what might happen if the search for love depends entirely on a woman's own resources, initiative, and work ethic. More to the point, Lesley Friedman's search suggests why courtship systems exist in the first place. They provide social rules and support for the mating search so that women don't have to manage their search all on their own. Also, if carried too far, the work-oriented, time-pressured nature of the search could extinguish love altogether. In the romantic tradition, love is anti-work. The ideology of romantic love and courtship had origins in the world of leisure. It took shape in the midst of a medieval court society where unmarried young men had time to engage in the pursuit of an unattainable woman. Moreover, as the romantic love ideology evolved into the courtship practices of 18th-century English society, there were new leisure opportunities created for the young to mate and marry. And even in very recent times, the school-based dating culture continued the tradition of romantic love as a leisure pursuit. College students work hard at their studies, and often at jobs as well, but they still remain one of the more leisured groups among adults under the age of 65.

Also, love offers respite from the world of work. It creates a place where the workplace values and expectations cannot intrude. It establishes a realm of leisure and privacy set apart from the world that consumes so much of our time, thought, and energy. Indeed, the very values traditionally associated with love stand in opposition to work. Love is indolent and inefficient. It is careless with time. Love has no billable hours. And romantic love flourishes in the midst of leisure. This is why all the personal ad placers, who are trying to save time and expand their prospects, still conjure a romantic vision of "walks on the beach," lazy evenings in front of the fire with a bottle of Merlot, and talking until the sun comes up. That is why the hyperachieving women, with triple Ivy degrees, still want to ditch their Palm Pilots in order to spend endless hours with a chosen beloved. This is why divas, the most driven and successful women in society, seek a private domestic life as the capstone to their career and why Barbra Streisand and Gloria Steinem devote their late middle age to building a bower of married domesticity.

Similarly, the classical attributes of love are anti-work. Love can inspire grandiosity and despair, languor and action, befuddlement and brilliant clarity, all at the same time. And love has its gentler moments. It can be patient, kind, and forgiving. Work, on the other hand, avoids emotionalism. It follows principles of rationality, efficiency, and productivity. It judges merit on the basis of performance. But it has no charity or forgiveness in its evaluation of performance; it can be cruel and harsh in its judgment.

For high-achieving women, love can offer a respite from perfectionism and performance anxieties. If you are truly loved, you can feel valued and cherished, no matter what happens at work. You are able to resist the constant pressure to compete, perform, and exceed expectations. You can have another life apart from your work life, where you are not subject to the same critical, judging, and evaluating scrutiny that you face every day in the workplace, or in the singles dating culture.

According to the personal ad postings on the elite sites, what busy, hyperachieving women are looking for is a romantic partner with whom they can spend a lot of leisure time. Although they seek a man who is an educated professional, as they are, they also want him to be available for intimacy and leisurely pleasures. In fact, their romantic fantasies seem to revolve around time rather than sex or even love: several express a wistful desire for a slower pace and cozy domesticity. A Harvard JD/MBA describes herself as a "pretty domestic goddess trapped in the body of a career woman." A Harvard AB with a Columbia JD '88 muses: "I dream of a guy who will give me a hug and a kiss while I'm cooking a feast for friends." Yet another says: "I spent too many years of my life traveling . . . I crave romance." For the new single woman, the challenge is to save time in order to make time for love.

CONFRONTING THE COURTSHIP CRISIS

THE ROMANTIC PLIGHT OF TODAY'S new single woman is the result of a contemporary crisis in dating and mating. This crisis has left many smart, successful, and otherwise happy young women in a state of perplexity about their love lives. They are frustrated by the dating scene, bewildered about how to go about finding the right man at the right time in their lives, and uncertain about their chances for love.

Until very recently, the social world has been unresponsive to their plight. In nearly every other domain, it has been attentive to the new single woman and supportive of her early life pursuits. But it has offered little support or sympathy for her desire to make a successful choice of a life partner. Indeed, the task of choosing the person one will spend one's life with, once an activity surrounded by social codes, sponsors, and rituals, is now chiefly a do-it-yourself project.

Even the few social thinkers who have been mindful of the romantic desires of young women have failed to offer a plausible solution to their plight. They've simply advised women to return to the past century's pattern of early marriage. Given the current patterns of higher education and early career development for both men and women, this seems unlikely to happen. To be sure, some women still marry shortly after college. But the shift to an older age at first marriage for the majority of college-educated women probably is here to stay.

If there is an answer to the contemporary crisis in courtship, it is not likely to be found in a wholesale return to early marriage. Nor does it seem appropriate to call for the kinds of legal and public policy measures that have been so effective in opening up opportunities for women in their school and work lives. Rather, the answer will likely be found in the ability of the society and the culture and the market to come up with innovative practices that fit the new realities of young women's lives and timetables.

In just the last few years, a number of new approaches to dating and mating have emerged. Many of the innovations originate in the marketplace. The Internet has opened up a whole new world of possibilities for mate selection. As it develops and matures, it could play an even larger and perhaps more effective role in matchmaking. There has also been innovation in the offline world. Introduction services such as *It's Just Lunch* and *Great Expectations*, the growth of personal ads in city newspapers and magazines, the advent of adult education workshops on how to find a mate, and the appearance of private dating coaches are all recent responses to the courtship crisis.

The social world outside the marketplace has been slower to respond, but there are changes going on there as well. One of the most significant is the growing role of friendship groups in the lives of young working singles. Friends are taking the place of parents as influential third parties in the mate selection process. Working singles often live far from their families and the communities where they grew up or went to college. Moreover, because they are older and more independent, they are less likely to rely on their parents' advice or active involvement in their romantic lives. At the same time, however, many are turning to friends for advice, support, and, every so often, consolation.

Of course, this is not entirely new. What is new, however, is that today's young adults have cultivated the art and practice of friendship to an extraordinary degree. Their notable success in this realm of intimacy no doubt owes something to the time they spend as singles before they marry. In the past, when people married shortly after they left school, they often grew apart from their crowd of high school and college friends. They spent their time on their relationships with spouse and children. Their social life revolved around their own family and other married couples. Today, however, when people stay single for a longer time, their friendships last well past college days and continue to develop and deepen over time. Friends, male and female, gay and straight, become like family. In cities, friends cluster in kinlike groups, or what author Ethan Watters has termed, "urban tribes."

To be sure, these early and hopeful social stirrings hardly add up to a new courtship system. But if a new system does develop, it is likely to emerge from the scattered, voluntary, imaginative, problem-solving efforts of many different groups of people, mainly acting independently of each other, who see opportunity—and perhaps some profit—in responding to some aspect of the crisis. Creative marketers will likely lead the way. In the meantime, it is useful to identify the features that might best distinguish a courtship system for the new single woman. Thus, if and when these features appear, they can be recognized and supported. Ideally, a new courtship system would include the following ideas.

IT WOULD FIT THE NEW SINGLE WOMAN'S TIMETABLE

THE PURSUIT OF EDUCATION AND early career development before marriage is a pattern that is rooted in broad social and economic changes. Like it or not, marriage today is untrustworthy as a form of economic or social security for women. In a society with a high divorce rate, women must be able to achieve economic self-sufficiency and social independence, and the path to these goals lies in personal and social investment in education and career development. Moreover, the evidence suggests that the chances for marriage are *better* for well-educated women. Women with higher levels of educational attainment are now more likely to marry and to stay married than those who are less well educated. Finally, beyond the economic benefits of a career, there is an intrinsic value in educational and career achievement. Finding rewarding work is essential to a fully realized adult life. Few would credibly argue that the answer to women's discontents in their love lives would be to roll back the advances that women have made in their work lives.

For the new single woman, the prime time for finding a marriage partner no longer predictably occurs during or shortly after the college years. It occurs at a later time—after the mid-20s and into the 30s or even 40s. Because the new single woman is likely to begin a serious search for a marriage partner later than women in the past, she has a shorter window of time to accomplish her goals—especially if she wants to have marriage-and-children. So in order to fit the new single woman's childbearing years, the practices and conventions of a contemporary courtship system should favor her time frame.

IT WOULD PROVIDE SOCIAL SUPPORT AND SYMPATHY FOR THE NEW SINGLE WOMAN'S AMBITIONS FOR MARRIAGE

AFTER THE COLLEGE YEARS, it is harder for working single women to meet and mix with single peer men. Such men are no longer densely concentrated in a small geographic space as they were on campus. They are spread out across a larger area. Consequently, the challenge is to create more social occasions and opportunities for women to meet a wide number of suitable single men.

One way to do so would be to encourage more third parties to be supportive of, and tactfully involved in, creating such occasions. For example, it would be helpful to widen the circle of sociability beyond the peer group or "tribe." We live at a time when some forms of sociability have been declining. Private entertaining at home has given way to home entertainment systems. People have less time for or interest in giving dinner parties or other social get-togethers that provide occasions for singles to meet new people. Singles and marrieds often socialize separately. Except for family reunions, weddings, and funerals, intergenerational gatherings are rare in many people's lives today. The social introduction has turned into a commercial "introduction service." To be sure, these new businesses are filling a very important niche in the dating world, but they should complement rather than replace the more traditional introduction services provided by family, friends, work acquaintances, and other people in one's social circle. These third parties are still the best sources of reliable background information on the single men they introduce to their female relatives and friends.

IT WOULD MAKE SENSE OF COHABITATION

AS IT NOW EXISTS, COHABITATION is an ambiguous form of romantic partnership. It serves several different, and often contradictory, purposes. It is both a pathway into marriage and an alternative to marriage. It can lead toward commitment and it can lead away from commitment. It can be advantageous at one stage in the early adult years and disadvantageous at another stage. Given its central place in the relationships system, it contributes to the ambiguity and confusion that beset the marriage-minded woman. It is hard for her to know whether a cohabiting partnership is a step in the progression toward commitment or a loop in the relationships cycle.

Some scholars have suggested that cohabitation-as-courtship might be distinguished from other kinds of cohabitation by recognizing it as part of a betrothal process.[1] For example, there might be formal religious recognition of a cohabiting couple's intention to enter into a process of marriage preparation. There might be some kind of public or family announcement of the union as a pre-engagement engagement. Special workshops and courses, both secular and religious, might be designed for cohabiting couples who are thinking about marriage. There are some creative ideas from the marketplace as well. The elegant Boston jewelry establishment, Shreve, Crump and Low, recently introduced "promise rings" for men to give to their chosen sweethearts as a step toward engagement. As the advertising copy suggests, the purchase of the "circlet of 18k gold or platinum set with a hint of diamond" is one way for a man to answer the "where is this relationship going" question. "You want to give her assurance that you definitely see a future together. But, for a variety of reasons, the time is simply not right to take to the bended knee. Enter the Promise Ring. . . . It is an ideal statement to your love interest and a warning to other would-be suitors that this hand is spoken for. . . . And when you are ready to take the next step, your Promise Ring will be taken in trade toward the purchase of an engagement ring." Without taking an eye off the bottom line, the jeweler helpfully casts the promise ring as a rung on a ladder of commitment.

IT WOULD RECOGNIZE THAT ROMANCE REQUIRES LEISURE

EARLIER ROMANTIC COURTSHIP systems allowed time for love. Indeed, the ideal of romantic courtship arose in the midst of a leisured court society. Later on, it flourished amidst balls, dinners, pump room conversations, card tables, and other social events in

18th-century society in England, and then still later, in middle class parlors and porches in 19th-century Anglo-American societies. By the mid-20th-century, romantic courtship had shifted into a youthful peer culture and to the relatively leisured social world of college students. On the campus, people had a convenient place and available time to party on the weekends, participate in club and social events, and hang out with their friends.

Today, however, many well-educated women are looking for marriage partners when they are out of school and working hard at full-time jobs. Romance has to be squeezed into work schedules, work-related travel, and the routine tasks of daily life. Moreover, the men women meet and fall in love with have their own hectic schedules and their own chosen cities. Also, there is a globalizing trend in mating and marrying. Some dating couples have to shuttle back and forth across continents to see each other at all.

Certain aspects of dating and mating do lend themselves to time-saving efficiencies. Most of them occur at the very beginning of a relationship, in the initial process of meeting and establishing mutual interest. But after this initial stage, there's good reason to throw efficiency to the winds and take time out for love.

IT WOULD PROVIDE A KNOWLEDGE BASE ON MATE SELECTION AND MARRIAGE

TODAY'S COLLEGE-EDUCATED YOUNG women are highly trained, conceptually and analytically sophisticated knowledge workers and meritocrats. In their work lives, they manage, manipulate, and interpret complicated data. When it comes to their love lives, it's a very different matter. Many of the smartest and most highly educated men and women in society today are mystified as to how to think about mate selection and how to make an intelligent choice. They have to glean whatever knowledge they can from whatever sources are handy—usually tabloids, television, and celebrity-themed magazines. To be sure, relationships books, workshops, tapes, and skills-training provide a source of information and self-help advice. But beyond these resources, they have little to go on. To some degree, this low level of knowledge reflects the relatively meager level of academic attention to these subjects. The study of marriage, and the empirical investigation of patterns of mate selection, have not been a top research topic in the academy for several decades. But it also reflects a more general social neglect and abdication of the responsibility to prepare and teach the next generation about this important life choice. In an economy that depends on knowledge, in a society that places such a high value on education and skills training, and in a polity that depends on the individual's capacity for reasoned judgments, it is all the more astonishing that there has been so little concern about transmitting a body of thought, knowledge, and skills on how to choose a mate for marriage, especially since the vast majority of young adults are likely to make that choice at some point in the not distant future.

This is not to suggest that a contemporary courtship system would adopt a standard curriculum on marriage or that it would promote the kind of mass messages that typified the courtship patterns of the mid-20th century. However, it does suggest that a courtship system must be grounded in a body of useful and reliable knowledge; that it must be relevant to young women's lives and to their romantic aspirations and goals; and that it should contribute to successful mate selection. To create this knowledge base, it will be necessary to treat the pursuit of lasting love as a subject of serious study and reflection and as a subject that requires the consultation of sources across a wide range of disciplines. The social sciences, history, art, literature, religion, and biology all have something to tell us about the means, ends, and delights of courtship.

But such knowledge can serve a purpose beyond the merely practical. It may revive the flagging faith that it is possible to find lasting love and that it is possible to integrate a loving marriage into a life of individual career achievement. Both love and work are central to adult life, as Freud famously said. Two successive generations of young, college-educated women have struggled to achieve and balance both. For baby boom women, the challenge came in the world of work. For today's young women, the challenge comes in the world of love.

N O T E S

Introduction: The Romantic Plight of
the New Single Woman

[1] Every year since 1976, the Monitoring the Future Survey conducted by the Institute for Social Research at the University of Michigan has asked a sample of high school seniors to rank the importance of 14 life goals. In 1992, 78 percent of respondents rated "having a good marriage and family life" as extremely important and at the top of their life goals, closely followed by "being able to find steady work" (77 percent). For a fuller discussion of youth survey trends on marriage, see Norval D. Glenn, "Values, Attitudes and American Marriage," *Promises to Keep: Decline and Renewal of Marriage in America*, ed. David Popenoe, et al. (Lanham, Maryland: Rowman & Littlefield Publishers, 1996), 15–33.

[2] *Young Adults' Attitudes Toward Marriage*, The Gallup Organization, April 2001, unpublished report submitted to The National Marriage Project. This report is based on the findings of a nationally representative telephone survey of adults, 20 to 29 years, conducted from January 29–March 7, 2001. A total of 1,003 interviews were completed. Results based on the entire sample have a margin of error of plus or minus 4 percentage points at the 95 percent confidence level. Select findings from the survey are published in *State of Our Unions 2001* (New Brunswick: The National Marriage Project, 2001).

[3] *Young Adults' Attitudes Toward Marriage.*

[4] U.S. Bureau of the Census, *America's Families and Living Arrangements: Population Characteristics, 2000*, prepared by Jason

Fields, Current Population Reports P20-537 (Washington, D.C: June 2001), 9.

⁵Unpublished tabulations from the General Social Surveys by Norval D. Glenn.

⁶*America's Families and Living Arrangements*, 9.

⁷For women born in 1933–1942, for example, only 7 percent first lived with someone in a cohabiting relationship rather than in a marriage. For women born in 1963–1974, 64 percent lived with a romantic partner before marriage. Tom W. Smith, *The Emerging 21st Century Family*, GSS Social Change Report No. 42 (Chicago: National Opinion Research Center, University of Chicago, 1999), 23.

⁸*America's Families and Living Arrangements*, 11.

⁹Beth L. Bailey, *From Front Porch to Back Seat: Courtship in Twentieth-Century America*, Johns Hopkins Paperbacks edition (Baltimore: Johns Hopkins University Press, 1988), 8.

Chapter I: Dating Mr. Not Ready

¹Calculations by Robert J. Lacey, The Massachusetts Institute for Social and Economic Research, University of Massachusetts at Amherst. From Public Use Microdata Series (PUMS) sample of decennial census for 1960 and March Current Population Survey for 1999, 2000, 2001.

²*America's Families and Living Arrangements*, 9.

³Tim B. Heaton, "Factors Contributing to Increasing Marital Stability in the United States." *Journal of Family Issues* 23 (2002): 392–409. See also the discussion "Age At First Marriage: What's Best?" in *State of Our Unions*, 2001 (New Brunswick, The National Marriage Project, 2001).

⁴For one therapist's views, see Patricia Dalton, "Daughters of the Revolution," *Washington Post*, May 21, 2000, Bl.

⁵U.S. Bureau of the Census, Housing Vacancies and Homeownership Annual Statistics 2001: Table 15. http://www.census.gov/hhes/www/housing/hvs/annual01/ann01t15.html.

⁶Carol Wolper, *The Cigarette Girl* (New York: Riverhead Books, 1999), 3.

⁷Wolper, *The Cigarette Girl*, 5.

[8]David M. Buss, et al., "A Half Century of Mate Preferences: The Cultural Evolution of Values," *Journal of Marriage and the Family* 63 (May 2001): 491–503.

Chapter II: The "No Good Men" Plaint

[1]Tama Janowitz, *A Certain Age* (New York: Doubleday, 1999), 152–53.

[2]For African-American women, the "no good man" problem is far more than mere perception. It is rooted in historical and cultural conditions that differ in important ways from those experienced by women of other ethnicities. The impact of slavery, racism, imprisonment, discrimination, economic injustice, and especially the lack of educational and job opportunity for African-American males, along with more recent cultural changes in attitudes toward sex, childbearing, and marriage, have contributed to a shortage of marriage-eligible Black men and a sharp decline in marriage within the African-American community. Compared to other women, African-American women are less likely to ever marry, less likely to have their cohabiting partnerships lead into marriage, more likely to have their marriages end in separation or divorce, and less likely to remarry. Though this important story is beyond the scope of this book, it has been brilliantly told by Orlando Patterson in *Rituals of Blood: Consequences of Slavery in Two American Centuries* (Washington, D.C.: Civitas Counterpoint, 1998). For his discussion of recent changes in marrying behavior, see especially 53–167.

[3]"Too Late for Prince Charming?," *Newsweek*, June 2, 1986, 54-61.

[4]For an illuminating analysis of these dueling demographic studies, and the media response to them, see Andrew Cherlin, "The Strange Career of the 'Harvard-Yale Study'," *Public Opinion Quarterly*, 54 (1990), 117–124.

[5]Joshua R. Goldstein and Catherine T. Kenney, "Marriage Delayed or Marriage Forgone? New Cohort Forecasts of First Marriage for U.S. Women," *American Sociological Review*, 66 (August 2001), 506–519, 517. Because of small sample size, the researchers note, it was not possible to project the chances of marriage for Black women, but the current data suggest that Black female college graduates are marrying at higher levels than Black women without college educations.

[6] U.S. Bureau of the Census, "Number, Timing and Duration of Marriages and Divorces: 1996," prepared by Rose M. Kreider and Jason M. Fields, Current Population Reports P70-80 (Washington, D.C: February 2002), 8.

[7] Pam Houston, *Cowboys Are My Weakness* (New York: W.W. Norton & Company, 1992; New York: Washington Square Press, 1993), 16.

[8] Pam Houston, *Waltzing the Cat* (New York: W.W. Norton & Company, 1998; New York: Washington Square Press, 1999), 219.

[9] *Waltzing the Cat*, 113.

[10] *Cowboys Are My Weakness*, A Reading Group Guide, n.p.

[11] Amy Sohn, *Run Catch Kiss* (New York: Simon & Schuster, 1999).

[12] Candace Bushnell, *Sex and the City* (New York: Atlantic Monthly Press, 1996: New York: Abacus, 1997), 29.

[13] Lucinda Rosenfeld, *What She Saw* (New York: Random House, 2000), 131.

[14] Laura Zigman, *Animal Husbandry* (New York: Dial Press, 1998).

[15] *What She Saw*, 269.

[16] U.S. Census, "Number, Timing and Duration of Marriages and Divorces: 1996," 14–15.

Chapter III: The New Single Woman

[1] U.S. Department of Education, *The Condition of Education 2001*, Table 26-2. "Immediate Transition to College." http://nces.ed.gov. After 1976, the percentage of high school graduates who went straight on to college fluctuated narrowly between male and female majorities. By the 1990s, women were in the majority of high school graduates who went directly to college, with the sole exception of the high school class of 1995.

[2] U.S. Department of Education, *Digest of Education Statistics 2000*, Table 173, "Total fall enrollment in degree-granting institutions, by attendance status, sex of student and control of institution: 1947–1998," http://neces.ed.gov.

[3] U.S. Department of Education, *Digest of Education Statistics 2000*, Table 248, "Earned degrees conferred by degree-granting institutions, by level of degree and sex of student": 1869–70 to 2009–10, http://nces.ed.gov.

[4] U.S. Department of Education, *Digest of Education Statistics 2000*, Table 248.

[5] Brendan I. Koerner, "Where the Boys Aren't," *U.S. News & World Report*, February 8, 1999, 47-55, 48.

[6] http://vpf-web.harvard.edu/factbook/current-facts http://www.dartmouth.edu/~oir/factbook.

[7] National Center for Educational Statistics "Competing Choices: Men and Women's Paths After Earning a Bachelor's Degree," prepared by Michael S. Clune, Anne-Marie Nunez, and Susan P. Choy, *Education Statistics Quarterly* (Washington, D.C.: GPO, 2001), 1–7, http://nces.edu.gove/pubs2002/quarterly/fall/q4–5.asp.

[8] "Study Abroad by U.S. Students, 1999–2000," *The Chronicle of Higher Education*, November 16, 2001, A 45.

[9] Laura Freschi, "No Boys Allowed," *Washingtonian*, November 2001, 163-68.

[10] Tamar Lewin, "Questions for Advanced Placement," *New York Times*, April 17, 2002, A16.

[11] The College Board, Participation in AP: Women, http://apcentral.collegeboard.com/article/0,1281,150-156-0-2060,00.html.

[12] National Coalition of Girls Schools, http:///www.ncgs.org/pages/news.htm.

[13] Tamar Lewin, "Girls' Schools Gain, Saying Coed Isn't Coequal," *The New York Times*, April 11, 1999, A1, 34.

[14] National Coalition of Girls Schools, http://www.ncgs.org/pages/news.htm.

[15] Tamar Lewin, "Girls' Schools Gain, 34.

[16] Joan Jacobs Brumberg, *The Body Project: An Intimate History of American Girls* (New York: Random House, 1997), 142.

[17] R. Kelly Raley, "Recent Trends and Differentials in Marriage and Cohabitation," *The Ties That Bind: Perspectives on Marriage and Cohabitation*, Linda J. Waite, ed (New York: Aldine de Gruyter, 2000), 32.

[18] Edward O. Laumann, et al, *The Social Organization of Sexuality: Sexual Practices in the United States* (Chicago: The University of Chicago Press, 1994), 189.

[19] Robert T. Michael, et al., *Sex in America: A Definitive Survey* (New York: Little, Brown and Company, 1994), 104.

[20] U.S. Bureau of the Census, "Number, Timing and Duration of

Marriages and Divorces: 1996," 17. See also discussion "What Are Your Chances of Divorce?" in *State of Our Unions 2002*, 25.

[21] Here, for example, is the advice that former Texas governor, Ann Richards, gave to a graduating class of high school girls: "Prince Charming may be driving a Honda and telling you you have no equal, but that's not going to do much good when you've got kids and a mortgage and, I might add, he's got a beer gut and a wandering eye."

[22] Women's Sports Foundation, Title IX: What Is It?, http://www.womenssportsfoundation.org.

[23] President's Council on Physical Fitness and Sports, *Physical Activity and Sport in the Lives of Girls: Physical and Mental Health Dimensions from an Interdisciplinary Approach* (Washington, D.C.: GPO, 1997), 21.

[24] Women's Sports Foundation, *Significant Events in Women's Sports History Post Title IX History*.

[25] Jere Longman, *The Girls of Summer: The U.S. Women's Soccer Team and How It Changed the World* (New York: HarperCollins, 2000, First Perennial Edition, 2001), 18.

[26] "Why It Was More Than a Game," *Time*, July 19, 1999, 64.

[27] Laura Elliott, "Here Comes Mia," *Washingtonian*, March 2001, 46–52, 49.

[28] See discussion in President's Council on Physical Fitness and Sports, *Physical Activity and Sport in the Lives of Girls*, 50–52.

[29] President's Council on Physical Fitness and Sports, *Physical Activity and Sport in the Lives of Girls*, 14–15.

[30] Sylvia Rimm, *See Jane Win: The Rimm Report on How 1,000 Girls Became Successful Women* (New York: Crown Publishers, 1999), 141.

[31] Jere Longman, *The Girls of Summer*, 26.

[32] Girls Scouts of the USA, *2000 Annual Report*, 10. http://www.girlscouts.org.

[33] Jane Gottesman, *Game Face: What Does a Female Athlete Look Like?* (New York: Random House, 2001).

[34] Therese Kauchak, *Good Sports: Winning, Losing, and Everything in Between* (Middleton, WI: Pleasant Company, 1999), 48.

[35] Phyllis Lehrer, "Renaissance Girl," *Amherst Bulletin*, February 15, 2002, 1.

Chapter IV: The Rise of a Relationships System

[1] Lawrence Stone, *The Family, Sex and Marriage in England 1500–1800* (New York: Harper & Row, 1977; New York: Harper Torchbooks, 1979), 213.

[2] Claire Tomalin, *Jane Austen: A Life* (New York: Random House, 1997; New York, Vintage Books, 1999), 102.

[3] For an analysis of the "soul mate" ideal, see *The State of Our Unions, 2000* (New Brunswick: National Marriage Project, 2000).

[4] Between 1970-95, for example, the percentage of divorced men who remarry has dropped from 86 to 78 percent in the same 25-year period; for divorced women, the percentage declines from 80.2 to 68.7. The percentage of life spent never married has increased from 35 to 46.5 percent for men and 30.6 to 39.8 percent for women. Robert Schoen and Nicola Standish, "The Retrenchment of Marriage: Results from Marital Status Life Table for the United States," 1995, unpublished manuscript. Department of Sociology, Pennsylvania State University, University Park, PA.

[5] Schoen and Standish, "Retrenchment," unpub. ms.

[6] Diane Daniel, "Signs of the Dating Times," *Boston Globe*, June 3, 2002, D15.

[7] William J. Goode, "The Theoretical Importance of Love," *American Sociological Review*, 24 (1959): 38–47.

[8] Arnold Van Gennep, *The Rites of Passage* (Chicago: University of Chicago Press, 1960), 175–76.

[9] Lois Smith Brady, "Vows," *New York Times*, December 29, 1996, 37.

[10] Lois Smith Brady, "Vows," *New York Times*, January 12, 1997, 37.

[11] Sherri Daley, "Twenty-five for a week: Going undercover as a Gen-Xer," *More*, March 2001, 104–7.

[12] Lynn Schnurnberger, "Have I Got a Girl for You!", *More*, April 2001, 55-57.

[13] (New York: The Macmillan Company, 1962), 276.

[14] U.S. Bureau of the Census, Number, Timing and Duration of Marriages and Divorces, 1.

[15] U.S. Bureau of the Census, Number, Timing and Duration of Marriages and Divorces, 11.

[16] Pamela Paul, *The Starter Marriage and the Future of Matrimony* (New York: Villard, 2001).

[17] Laumann et al., *Social Organization of Sexuality*, 329.

[18] Bailey, *Front Porch*, 45.

[19] Paula Fass, *The Damned and the Beautiful: American Youth in the 1920s* (New York: Oxford University Press, 1977; New York, Oxford University Press paperback, 1979), 276. The study I have cited from Fass was conducted in the late 1930s by the noted sociologists Ernest Burgess and Paul Wallin. It was one of the first reliable studies of sexual behavior among engaged college students. However, as Fass notes, these patterns reflect the liberalization of sexual morality on coed college campuses that began to take hold in the 1920s and continued thereafter. This increased likelihood of premarital sex among engaged college couples did not change much in the ensuing decades. The connection between premarital sex and engagement remained a fairly stable feature of college relationships through the 1950s and early 1960s until the sexual revolution hit the campuses in the mid-1960s.

[20] Cited in Bailey, *Front Porch*, 143.

[21] Arthur Levine and Jeanette S. Cureton, *When Hope and Fear Collide: A Portrait of Today's College Student* (San Francisco: Jossey Bass, 1998), 109.

[22] Levine and Cureton, Hope and Fear, 111-12.

[23] U.S. Bureau of the Census, Married Couple and Unmarried-Partner Households: 2000, Census 2000 Special Reports (Washington, D.C., 2000), 3.

[24] Popenoe and Whitehead, *Should We Live Together?*, 3.

[25] Two fast-growing types, not considered here, are the cohabiting union with children and the cohabiting union involving older couples who live together in order to avoid legal entanglements and complications in taxes, inheritance, pension, and social security benefits. Unmarried opposite sex couples 65 and older rose 73 percent from 1990 to 1999, according to *Modern Maturity*, the magazine of the AARP. See Galina Espinoza, "There Goes the Bride," *Modern Maturity*, July/August 2002, 13.

[26] Pamela J. Smock, "Cohabitation in the United States: An Appraisal of Research Themes, Findings, and Implications," *Annual Review of Sociology* 26: (2000), 1–20, 3.

[27] The relatively short duration of many youthful cohabiting partnerships and their outcome—either ending in a breakup or leading to marriage—is another clue that American cohabitation functions more like courtship than as a marriage alternative.

[28] Katherine Shaver, "On Congrested Roads, Love Runs Out of Gas," *Washington Post*, June 3, 2002, B1.

[29] Geeta Anand, "ID Card Found in Trade Center's Ruins Brings Love Story to Sad End," *Wall Street Journal*, September 20, 2001, B1.

[30] Irene Sege, "Meet Leslie Boorse," *Boston Globe*, October 25, 1998, A1.

[31] Irene Sege, "After Facing Fears, She Embarks on New Chances and Challenges," *Boston Globe*, October 31, 1998, A1, A12. According to Sege, the reporter for this series, Leslie eventually got an answer. Reader, she married him.

[32] Jack Thomas, "Mixed Grades for 'Single Year' Series," *Boston Globe*, November 16, 1998, A15.

Chapter V: Should We Live Together?

[1] Estimates of the percentage of cohabiting partnerships that lead into marriage vary, depending on the data source and on whether the partnerships are first-time cohabitations or all cohabitations. For all cohabiting unions, "the most recent estimates suggest that about 55 percent of cohabiting couples marry and 40 percent end the relationship within five years of the beginning of the cohabitation." Smock, "Cohabitation in the United States," 3. For first cohabiting unions, a recent report by the Centers for Disease Control estimates, "58 percent of cohabitations that have lasted at least 3 years have made the transition to marriage by that time and 70 percent of cohabitations that have lasted for 5 years have made the transition to marriage by that time." The CDC report also notes that the probability that a first cohabiting union becomes a marriage within 5 years is higher for White women (75 percent) than for Hispanic (61 percent) or Black women (48 percent). Bramlett, Matthew D., and William D. Mosher, *Cohabitation, Marriage, Divorce and Remarriage in the United States*, National Center for Health Statistics, Vital Health Statistics, series 23, no 22 (Washington, D.C.: GPO, 2002), 1–93, 12.

[2] Quoted in *Marriage—Just a Piece of Paper?*, Katherine Anderson, Don Browning, Brian Boyer, eds. (Grand Rapids, MI: Wm. B. Eerdmans Publishing Co., 2000), 164.

[3] Stein Ringen, *The Family in Question* (London: Demos, 1998), 47.

[4] Catherine A. Surra and Christine R. Gray, "A Typology of Processes of Commitment to Marriage," *Ties That Bind*, 260.

[5] *State of Our Unions 2002*, 12.

[6] U.S. Bureau of the Census, "America's Families and Living Arrangements," 10–11.

[7] Frances Goldscheider and Calvin Goldscheider, *The Changing Transition to Adulthood: Leaving and Returning Home* (Thousand Oaks, CA: Sage Publications, 1999), 139.

Chapter VI: The Search Begins

[1] Quoted in Norval Glenn and Elizabeth Marquardt, *Hooking Up, Hanging Out, and Hoping for Mr. Right: College Women on Dating and Mating Today* (New York: Institute for American Values, 2001), 48.

[2] The data points for this line graph are drawn from the March Current Population Surveys for three successive years: 1999, 2000, and 2001. It is important to know what this figure shows and does not show. It does not follow one birth year cohort of women as it moves through the years from 22 to 41. Rather, it indicates the marital status, for one time period, of 20 separate birth-year cohorts of college-educated women. Thus the points representing women who are 25 and women who are 30 reflect the experience of different groups of individuals, born five years apart.

[3] Calculations by Robert J. Lacey, 1960 PUMS.

[4] www.washingtonpost.cm/wp-srv/entertainment/lovelife/features/lovelife 1008.htm, November 10, 1999.

[5] Lois Smith Brady, "Vows", *New York Times*, March 24, 1996, 57.

[6] Lois Smith Brady, "Vows," *New York Times*, January 16, 2000, 7.

[7] Lois Smith Brady, "Vows," *New York Times*, April 16, 2000, 11.

[8] Lois Smith Brady, "Vows," *New York Times*, February 17, 2002, 11.

[9] Lois Smith Brady, "Vows," *New York Times*, November 19, 2000, 11.

[10] Lois Smith Brady, "Vows," *New York Times*, January 23, 2000, 7.

[11] Lois Smith Brady, *Love Lessons: Twelve Real-Life Love Stories* (New York: Simon & Schuster, 1999), 98.

[12] Brady, *Love Lessons*, 21.

[13] Brady, *Love Lessons*, 97.

Chapter VII: Working at Love

[1] Ellen Fein and Sherrie Schneider, *The Rules: Time-Tested Secrets for Capturing the Heart of Mr. Right* (New York: Warner Books, 1995; New York, Warner Books Paperback, 1996), 49.

[2] Fein and Schneider, *The Rules*, 3.

[3] Fein and Schneider, *The Rules*, 2.

[4] Bonnie Rothman Morris, "You've Got Romance! Seeking Love on Line," *New York Times*, Thursday, August 26,1999, E1.

[5] Bob Tedeschi, E-Commerce Report, *New York Times*, February 4, 2002, C6.

[6] One noteworthy exception: The *New York Review of Books* ran back-of-the-book personal ads catering to an urbane class of smoking, talking, and drinking left-wing intellectuals whose lives and loves were much romanticized and admired by history and English graduate students in the 1960s.

[7] The Right Stuff lists: Amherst, Barnard, Bowdoin, Brown, Bryn Mawr, Caltech, Cambridge University, Claremont Colleges, Columbia, Cornell, Dartmouth, Davidson, Duke, Emory, Harvard, Haverford, Johns Hopkins, Juilliard, McGill, Medical Schools, Middlebury, MIT, Mount Holyoke, Northwestern, Oberlin, Oxford, Penn, Princeton, Queen's University, Radcliffe, Reed, RISD, Rice, Smith, Stanford, Swarthmore, University of California at Berkeley, University of Chicago.

[8] Joshua Kurlantzick, "Hello, goodbye, hey maybe I love you?" *U.S. News and World Report*, June 4, 2001, 43.

[9] December 16, 1998, A1.

Conclusion: Confronting the Courtship Crisis

[1] See Michael G. Lawler, "Becoming Married in the Catholic Church: A Traditional Post-Modern Proposal," INTAM review, 7 (2001a), 37-54, for one theologian's well-argued proposal for church recognition of cohabitation as part of a marriage process.

INDEX

Teresa A. B. Gauthier

ABOUT THE AUTHOR

Award-winning journalist BARBARA DAFOE WHITEHEAD writes about social issues for numerous national publications. She holds a Ph.D. in American social history from the University of Chicago and currently serves as the codirector of the National Marriage Project at Rutgers University. She is the author of *The Divorce Culture*. She lives in Amherst, Massachusetts.

Printed in the United States
by Baker & Taylor Publisher Services